The Disciple's Journal

Presented To:

_____

CHRIST IN YOUTH

Christ In Youth is a not-for-profit ministry introducing youth to a saving knowledge
of Jesus Christ, equipping and motivating them to share their faith in Christ with others.
This mission is accomplished through short-term mission trips to urban and international
destinations, Winter Ski Conferences, Summer Conferences, weekend Discipleship
retreats, Believe junior high conventions, and the National Youth Leaders Convention.
For more information about our programs or other resources, please contact us at:

Christ In Youth, Box B, Joplin, MO 64802
Phone (417) 781-2273 Fax (417) 781-5958
E-mail resources@ciy.com
Order toll free 1-877-200-4336
Visit our web site at: www.ciy.com/resources

Change Youth...Change The World!

Published by: Christian Outfitters, 301 Hunterview Drive, Granbury, Texas 76048

Printed in the United States of America
January 2001
Fourth Edition

Scripture taken from the Holy Bible, New International Version. Copyright 1973, 1978,
1984 International Bible Society. Used by permission of Zondervan Bible Publishers. All
other Scripture quotations in this publication are from the King James Version (KJV). Public
domain.

ISBN 0-9651908-0-3

© Copyright 1995 by Douglas Morrell and Jon Dean Smith, Christian Outfitters, Inc. All
rights reserved including the right of reproduction in whole or in part in any form.
Reproduction or translation of any part of this work beyond permitted by Section 107 or 108
of the 1976 United States Copyright Act without the permission of the copyright owner is
unlawful according to our Lord and by the government. Requests for permission or further
information should be addressed to Christian Outfitters, 301 Hunterview Drive, Granbury,
Texas 76048.

Discipleship Is An Adventure. We Outfit The Saints For The Journey
301 Hunterview Drive • Granbury, Texas 76048
www.christianoutfitters.com
outfitters@christianoutfitters.com

Seasoned travelers keep journals as reminders of events, places and people they have encountered along the way. As believers, we are sojourners with a more important destination and purpose. Heaven is our destination. Our goal is to become like Christ. Our pilgrimage is a rugged adventure through unfamiliar wilderness filled with difficulty, risk and surprise. Along the path, God reveals His character to show us our need. In this process called discipleship, we are formed, conformed and transformed into His Son's image. Over the years, we've searched for a journal that would provide a place for dedicated Bible meditation, daily journaling and prayer communion with God. We were unsuccessful, so after much prayer and work, we designed the first comprehensive Disciple's Journal. A book made for long walks in the wilderness.

From experience, we've learned to use all the tools contained in this Journal. These have provided the foundation from which God shows us our need. This scripture-filled one-on-one partnering produces fruit that lasts.

We hope you discover the Disciple's Journal to be a valuable tool to assist you as you travel along your journey. It's not something we take lightly. It's serious. But your guide, the Holy Spirit, is with you. He knows the way and has led countless thousands through before. Down the trail there are wonderful and fascinating adventures to embrace. Do so with zeal and with the heart of a warrior. Nothing less will do. Most importantly, enjoy the trip as you go. Every turn in the road. Each new experience. As you go, record your thoughts. You'll find, as we have, that the Journal becomes an indispensable companion. Adventure awaits.

The Journal contains five keys with corresponding icons. Together, these five elements will help outfit you for your journey. Youth groups, home groups, cell groups, adult groups, family or friends will benefit from its application.

 a weekly character study or the commands/promises of Jesus,

 a daily journal entry section,

 the words of wisdom,

 the daily instruction of Jesus,

 and prayer needs, teaching notes & accountability checklist.

The Disciple's Journal
A One Year Guide For Believers
Being Conformed To His Image

Discipleship

The Real Journey Begins:
Disciples are made and not ready-made. In most circles of Christianity you can be a tourist, but if you cross the bridge to discipleship, you become an explorer. That's because discipling is a lost art. And, just like discovering a key that unlocks the door to knowledge of the language and literature of ancient Egypt, it's what Jesus did first. Most of today's seminary graduates are versed in academics, but haven't spent time in a discipling environment. Like discovering the City of Ur, the master's plan of placing a seasoned instructor beside a willing student produces a wealth of experience and heritage.

The quest for real discipleship is a commitment to be like Jesus Christ. That means both acting as He did and being willing to accept the same treatment. It means facing a hostile world and doing it fearlessly. It means confessing before others that Jesus is Lord, and being confident that He will also speak on our behalf before the Father. This takes the heart of a warrior and the sensitivity of a lamb.

God's discipleship model is described in the pages of His Word. Basically, home should be base camp training and nurturing for children, while the church should be advanced training for the parents to carry out this mission. When the home partners with the church, consistent with Gods' discipleship plan, a map emerges capable of bringing forth men and women of integrity. As you travel through these pages, you will gain a fresh perspective of what God desires of you. Hopefully, you will become involved in the process of discipleship.

Why The Disciple's Journal:
In the last ten years I've traveled extensively, setting foot on many exciting spiritual continents and lots of challenging islands in between. The man who departs is never the man who returns. Inevitably, as I see through the eyes of Christ, something happens to me, and I just don't see the world, or myself, in the same way again. Steinbeck said, "We don't take a trip. A trip takes us." And once it takes us, it's ours forever.

Travel is experience. And the journey we are on is wonder. Experienced travelers know that travel isn't easy. It can be gritty, tough, demanding, upsetting. But I haven't yet taken a trip–or rather, a trip hasn't yet taken me–that wasn't worth it.

The Journal's Purpose:
The function of the Journal is to echo the purpose of the church… that each believer be built up into the likeness of Christ (formed, conformed and transformed). Disciplines such as prayer, study, solitude, simplicity, confession, and celebration involve formal means of training and can be realized throughout the Journal. In fact, you will never mature in the character of Christ unless you are actively involved in these daily disciplines. However, these acts in and of themselves do not make you acceptable to God. He accepts you on grace alone, and you are justified by grace alone. These disciplines provide a place for your spiritual adventure, "train yourself in godliness," (1 Tim. 4:7). The only way to free your mind and body from destructive habits is through proper discipline. You are in essence, "training for reigning." As an exercise in building faith–as you begin to recognize God for who He is and who you are in relationship to Him–you begin to place things into perspective. You are totally dependent upon God for everything. These exercises nurture you into the correct vertical relationship with God, and as a result, a right relationship with those around you.

Godly Men and Women Journal:
The Bible is filled with examples of successful journal writers. Journaling is a record of your spiritual journey. You will find it to be one of the most effective ways to discipline yourself and maintain a daily dialogue with Jesus. Remember this, keeping a journal is not just for writers. Anyone can learn how to do it and enjoy it. As you write, you'll discover what is truly in your heart. When you reread your journal (or when your children's children do), you will once again encounter people and places who have been instrumental in shaping your life. Here are a few suggestions that will help you get the most out of keeping your Journal.

How To Start:
Be Honest. God is not shocked by truth. He desires it. Until you are honest with God about your innermost feelings–no matter how ugly–there can be no real discipleship.

Express Yourself. Don't write to impress anyone. Reveal your heart to God. The Journal is designed to encourage total freedom of expression without concern over formal rules of writing. So, scratch out words. Don't worry about grammar. Relax, have fun, and enjoy the Lord! Focus on exposing your heart, not on your writing skills.

Journal Formats:
- Story Format. This method involves writing down brief episodes from your daily life. They can include parts of actual conversations with others, descriptions of how you feel about events, your feelings, etc.
- List Format. This method captures quickly and concisely the events and emotions you experience during the day. Just write out a title like, "Thoughts I should keep from today," or "Things that are most important today," or "Things that tested my patience today," and then write out a few words beneath your topic. The possibilities are endless.

Journal Prompts:
Using either the story or the list format, *choose one* of the following and write as much or as little as you like, but **be honest!**
1. Close your eyes and "see" Jesus sitting across from you right now. What would you say to Him? Now write.
2. Write out one thing you've been afraid to tell Jesus. Then, tell Him why you've been afraid to talk to Him about it.
3. Meditate on a passage of scripture. As you do, write questions you don't understand. Then listen and write down what Jesus said.
4. Ask our Lord to tell you how to know Him better. Write down His response and make this your purpose throughout the day. At the end of the day, describe the experience.

Christ-Centered Principles:

Alertness vs. Unawareness
Awareness of what is going on around me and being prepared to respond in Christ's character. Mark 14:38

Attentiveness vs. Unconcern
Honoring a person above myself by giving them my full, undivided attention. Hebrews 2:1

Availability vs. Self-centeredness
Making my entire life secondary to those I am called to serve and build up in the Lord. Philippians 2:20-21

Boldness vs. Fearfulness
Having confidence, knowing that what I am doing or saying is empowered by God through the Holy Spirit. Acts 4:29

Cautiousness vs. Rashness
Moving in God's timing so that all I do achieves maximum success. Proverbs 19:2

Compassion vs. Indifference
Demonstrating love in my daily life by bearing other's suffering. I John 3:17

Contentment vs. Covetousness
Knowing that God has given everything I need today for true joy. I Timothy 6:8

Creativity vs. Under Achievement
Seeing everything as an opportunity for growth through God's perspective. Romans 12:2

Decisiveness vs. Double Mindedness
Making tough decisions based on God's Word, His Will and His Way. James 1:5

Deference vs. Rudeness
Respecting and honoring those around me to the degree that my freedom is limited. Romans 14:21

Dependability vs. Inconsistency
Honoring commitments and my word even when it is costly to do so. Psalm 15:4

Determination vs. Faint Heartedness
Regardless of opposition, purposing to accomplish God's desires in His timing. II Timothy 4:7-8

Diligence vs. Slothfulness
Seeing each task before me as given by Jesus and giving all my strength and energy to accomplish it. Colossians 3:23

Discernment vs. Judgment
Learning to think God's thoughts, esteeming what He esteems and despising what He despises. I Samuel 16:7

Discretion vs. Simple Mindedness
Making choices each day that bring honor to God. Proverbs 22:3

Endurance vs. Giving Up
Regardless of situation, living a life of faith knowing the certainty of victory. Galatians 6:9

Enthusiasm vs. Apathy
An outward expression of joy based on the inner peace of God. I Thessalonians 5:16, 19

Faith vs. Presumption
Having an established conviction regarding things God is doing and believing He will see it through based on His promises. Hebrews 11:1

Flexibility vs. Resistance
Setting my agenda each day on Christ's agenda, and not my own. Colossians 3:2

Forgiveness vs. Rejection
Erasing past offenses committed against me, knowing that my prayers for forgiveness are unanswered until I do. Ephesians 4:32

Generosity vs. Stinginess
Knowing that everything belongs to God and I am to use it as He instructs, to His glory. II Corinthians 9:6

Gentleness vs. Harshness
Cherishing and loving others as a loving mother does for her own. I Thessalonians 2:7

Gratefulness vs. Unthankfulness
Expressing to God and others that what they are doing is bringing me closer to Christ. I Corinthians 4:7

Hospitality vs. Loneliness
Joyfully opening my home and sharing my life with other believers. Hebrews 13:2

Keys To Living A Disciple's Life

Humility vs. Pride
Knowing that my accomplishments have come through God and others. James 4:6

Initiative vs. Unresponsiveness
Seeing what needs to be done and doing it before I am asked to do it. Romans 12:21

Joyfulness vs. Self Pity
Overflowing with the fruit of the Spirit each day so that true enthusiasm is realized. Psalm 16:11

Justice vs. Fairness
Adopting mercy, justice, humility and faithfulness as my core virtues. Micah 6:8

Loyalty vs. Unfaithfulness
Giving up the comforts, joys, and desires of my life in exchange for others. John 15:13

Love vs. Selfishness
Giving to others without hesitation knowing that I will not be repaid or profit in this world in any way. I Corinthians 13:3

Meekness vs. Anger
Realizing that my life is not my own and God is in control. Psalm 62:5

Obedience vs. Willfulness
Freedom to express myself in creative ways knowing that I am under the protection of God. II Corinthians 10:5

Orderliness vs. Disorganization
Maintaining everything around and about me so that

it is ready for God's immediate use when He desires. 1 Corinthians 14:40

Patience vs. Restlessness
Going through hardship with joy knowing that God is bringing about His promise in me. Romans 5:3-4

Persuasiveness vs. Contentiousness
Persuading others to believe, but doing so with kindness and gentleness. II Timothy 2:24

Punctuality vs. Tardiness
Honoring others and showing love by being on time as promised. Ecclesiastes 3:1

Resourcefulness vs. Wastefulness
Knowing that God tests my ability to receive true riches based on my use of material possessions. Luke 16:10

Responsibility vs. Unreliability
Doing what God and others expect of me. Romans 14:12

Reverence vs. Disrespect
Recognizing that my response, not the situation, is what God wants me to see so that I can become more like Jesus. Proverbs 23:17-18

Security vs. Anxiety
Keeping my sights and my efforts focused on eternal values and not the temporal. John 6:27

Self-Control vs. Self-Indulgence
Absolute obedience to the first prompting of God's Spirit. Galatians 5:24-25

Sensitivity vs. Callousness
Allowing God's Spirit to show me how I should respond to the feelings and needs of those around me. Romans 12:15

Sincerity vs. Hypocrisy
Sincerely loving others without having a hidden agenda. I Peter 1:22

Thriftiness vs. Extravagance
Maintaining godly stewardship and faithfulness in all things. Luke 16:11

Thoroughness vs. Incompleteness
Paying attention to the details knowing that I will not receive more until I am responsible with the little. Proverbs 18:15

Tolerance vs. Prejudice
Regardless of maturity, seeking to maintain unity with other believers in my thoughts, attitudes, love, spirit and purpose. Philippians 2:2

Truthfulness vs. Deception
Depositing into others the truthful reporting of events because it will yield future rewards. Ephesians 4:25

Virtue vs. Impurity
Being so obedient to God's Word and conformed to His character that others begin to see Him and not me. II Peter 1:5

Wisdom vs. Natural Inclinations
Viewing everything through God's global perspective and responding accordingly. Proverbs 9:10

Focused Prayer

In Prayer, Submission Is The Gateway To Receiving God's Fullest Blessings:
Jesus said, "Until now you have asked nothing in My name. Ask, and you will receive, that your joy may be full" (John 16:24). Jesus placed priority on prayer.

"The one concern of the Devil is to keep Christians from praying. He fears nothing from prayerless studies, prayerless work, and prayerless religion. He laughs at our toil, mocks at our wisdom, but trembles when we pray." Samuel Chadwick

1. **Prayer Principles (Gen. 18:17-33):**
    1. The absence of good, not the presence of evil, brings God's mercy.
    2. Praying must line up with God's character and His covenant with us.
    3. God saves by many or by few.
2. **An Intercessor's Heart (Ex. 32:11-14, 30-34):**
    1. Real character is revealed in time of crisis.
    2. Real love focuses on the concerns of others more than self.
    3. Prayer warriors stand in the gap between sin and God's wrath.
3. **Standing In The Gap (Josh. 10:12-14):**
    1. We must fight to possess God's promise.
    2. Satan wages war on those who stand for Christ.
    3. Prayerful victories produce faithful witness of God's strength.
4. **Powerful Intervention (Is. 36:1-37, 38):**
    1. Prayer prepares and sustains us through tribulations.
    2. Prayer destroys evil forces.
5. **Prayerful Leaders (Eph. 3:14-21):**
    1. Effective leaders pray.
    2. Effective ministry can only be accomplished through the Holy Spirit.
    3. Effective Christians are recognized by their inward character.
6. **Prayer Proves Our Faith (Acts 4:1-37):**
    1. Prayer overcomes persecution.
    2. Answered prayer confirms Christ's authority.
    3. Prayer brings about power and unity.
7. **God's Presence (1 Kings 8:22-61):**
    1. Be at peace with God, walk in His statutes, and keep His commandments.
    2. If we seek God, He is instantly with us.
    3. He will fill us whenever we make room for Him.

8. **The Key To Deliverance (Acts 12:1-17):**
   1. Sincere unceasing prayer is the key to deliverance.
   2. Believe that God hears and will answer your prayers.
9. **Not Your Will But His (1 John 5:14, 15):**
   1. Ask in Jesus' name according to His character and nature.
   2. Abide in Christ and allow His words to abide in you.
   3. Have faith.
   4. Be righteous in life and fervent in your prayer.

The Seven Steps Of Focused Prayer

"And when you pray, do not be like the hypocrites, for they love to pray standing in the synagogues and on the streetcorners to be seen by men. I tell you the truth, they have received their reward in full. But when you pray, go into your room, close the door and pray to your Father, who is unseen. Then your Father, who sees what is done in secret, will reward you. And when you pray, do not keep on babbling like pagans, for they think they will be heard because of their many words. Do not be like them, for your Father knows what you need before you ask him." This then is how you should pray: **(Matthew 6:19-33)**

1. **Our Father:** to begin, shared intimacy and recognition are expressed.

2. **Hallowed be Your name:** enter His presence through praise and worship

3. **Your kingdom come:** ask for the establishment of God's rule today in the lives and circumstances for yourself, your family, your church family, and the nation.

4. **Give us:** pray daily asking God to provide for all your needs.

5. **And forgive us:** ask God to forgive you knowing that God will only forgive our sins as we forgive others who have sinned against us.

6. **And do not lead us:** ask for God's strength to stand in His might. Put on the full armor of God. Pray a hedge of protection about yourself and your loved ones.

7. **For Yours is the kingdom:** thank God for sharing His kingdom, power and glory with you.

Weekly Character, Commands & Promises Study:

On the left side of alternating pages you'll first find a Discipleship Study (lessons 1-34) followed by the Commands & Promises (lessons 35-52) designed to help you discover and develop the character and instruction of Jesus. For the Character Studies:

A. Definition. Look up the word in a dictionary and copy the definition onto your study page.

B. Everyday Life Example. Relate the character quality to a situation in your life such as sports activities, social situations, family relationships, etc.

C. Positive Biblical Example. Read all the passages listed. Then summarize one of them. Don't try to tell the whole story; just tell how the character quality is demonstrated.

D. Negative Biblical Example. Follow the same procedure as you would for the positive example. This time tell how the character quality is lacking.

E. My Own Life. Sections A, B, C, and D will help you understand the character quality and bring the Scriptures to life. Now, apply this information to your own life. Before you try to answer the questions, stop and ask God to build this quality into your life.

- Answer the questions in as much detail as necessary. Only a few lines are provided on the study page, so use extra paper if you need more room to write.
- Design a project that will help to develop each character quality in your life. The project must include a goal and some practical steps to fulfill that goal. For instance, if you have been intending to repaint your room since last May, commit yourself to finishing the job by next month. You will learn more about Perseverance.
- A study of character qualities is of little value unless the qualities are actually built into your life. Study, by itself, will not do the job. You must experience God's power in your life to build character. That's why the projects are so important.

F. Memorization. Several verses are listed. Look up all the verses and choose the one that applies best to your life. Copy it carefully on the study sheet, word-for-word. Learn it word-for-word, memorizing the reference as well.

G. Self-evaluation. The questions in this section are designed to help you see areas in your life in which God has worked, or in which work needs to be done. Be very honest with yourself. Your success in your journal is not measured by "right" answers, but by the changes accomplished in your life. The more honest your answers, the more apt you are to make necessary changes. You do not need to write out answers, but spend some time just thinking.

Note: The study pages will usually require about sixty minutes to complete. You can either complete each page in one sitting or divide it over the week. Keeping a record of time spent on each lesson will not only encourage you to spend sufficient time each day before the Lord, but, when you finish this journal 12 months from now, you can look back and see how many hours you have invested in working toward God's goal for you: "Conformed to the image of his Son."

Words Of Wisdom:
There are 31 chapters in the Book of Proverbs. Each day read one chapter corresponding to the appropriate day of the month. Example: if today is the 23rd, read the entire 23rd chapter of Proverbs.

Daily Journal Entry:
This is not a diary. It is a Spiritual Journal. Jot down a few lines each day about what God is doing in your life. Over time, you will begin to see how God is at work in your life and all around you.

Christ's Commands & Instructions:
These are the Words Of Life. Make this your weekly purpose.

Prayer Requests:
Jot down your prayers, those for your family/friends, brothers & sisters in Christ, church/city/state/country and how God responds. You will learn that God cares for you and loves to spend time with you.

Lesson 1: Perseverance

A. Definition of perseverance: _____
_____

B. An example from my everyday life: _____
_____

C. A positive example from the Bible: Gen. 6:11-22; 29:22-28; Matt. 10:16-22; Heb. 12:1-
3. _____

D. A negative example from the Bible: Matt. 13:20-21; 26:69-75; 2 Tim. 4:9, 10. _____
_____

E. Thinking about perseverance in my own life:

1. When have I persevered? _____
_____

2. In what situation did I fail to persevere? _____
_____

3. What problem in my life could God use to build perseverance? _____
_____

4. Who can be a Christian model for me of perseverance? _____
_____

5. How can I develop this quality in my life? _____
_____

F. A scripture verse I will memorize to help build perseverance into my life: Matt.
24:13; Rom. 8:37; 1 Cor. 13:7; 15:58; 2 Tim. 2:3; Heb. 12:2; James 1:4. _____
_____

G. Self-evaluation:
1. Do I finish books I begin reading?
2. Can others depend on me to carry out an assignment to its completion?
3. Have I established clear goals for my spiritual life?
4. Am I able to set aside distractions in order to reach those goals?
5. Do I have a goal in life I am willing to die for?
6. Do my goals affect my daily life in a perceptible way?
7. Do I have negative examples of those who did not persevere that can be a warning to me?
8. Am I in control of my daily activities so that I do not bounce randomly from one activity to the next?
9. Have I considered what I want to be five years from now? Ten years from now?
10. Would people close to me consider me a persevering person?
11. How long can I go without yielding to temptation in an area of personal weakness?
12. Have I developed the habit of daily prayer?
13. How long have I gone without missing a day of reading Scripture and praying?
14. What appealing distractions have I given up in order to meet my personal goals?
15. Do pressures challenge me to motivation or do I feel like quitting when things get difficult?
16. Am I cooperating with the One who endured the cross to give me the spirit of endurance?

Day 1: _____

_____

_____

_____

_____

_____

_____

_____

_____

_____

_____

_____

_____

Day 2: _____

_____

_____

_____

_____

_____

_____

_____

_____

_____

_____

_____

_____

_____

_____

Day 3: _____

_____

_____

_____

_____

_____

_____

_____

_____

_____

_____

_____

_____

Words Of Wisdom: read a chapter from the Book of Proverbs corresponding with today's date (if today is the seventh, read chapter seven from the Book of Proverbs.)

He that has my commandments, and keeps them, is he that loves me: and he that loves me will be loved by my Father, and I will love him and reveal myself to him. John 14:21

Day 4: _____

_____
_____
_____
_____
_____
_____
_____
_____

Day 5: _____

_____
_____
_____
_____
_____
_____
_____
_____

Day 6: _____

_____
_____
_____
_____
_____
_____
_____
_____

Day 7: _____

_____
_____
_____
_____
_____
_____
_____
_____

Prayer Needs/Requests & How God Responded: _____

_____

_____

_____

_____

_____

_____

_____

_____

_____

_____

_____

_____

_____

_____

Notes From This Week's Fellowship/Teaching: _____

_____

_____

_____

_____

_____

_____

_____

_____

_____

_____

_____

_____

_____

_____

_____

_____

_____

_____

_____

_____

_____

_____

Personal Accountability Checklist: (if in a group, have someone else check you)

- ☐ I completed the character or command promise study.
- ☐ I read a chapter from the Book Of Proverbs each day.
- ☐ I journaled each day.

Lesson 2: Patience

A. Definition of patience: _____

_____

B. An example from my everyday life: _____

_____

C. **A positive example from the Bible:** Gen. 39:19-23; Job 1:13-22; Matt. 27:11-14; James 5:7-11. _____

D. **A negative example from the Bible:** Num. 20:1-12; 1 Sam. 13:8-14; Luke 10:38-42.

_____

E. **Thinking about patience in my own life:**

1. When have I clearly been patient? _____

_____

2. In what situation did I fail to be patient? _____

_____

3. What are some symptoms I display that show I am being impatient? _____

_____

4. What problem in my life could God use to build patience? _____

_____

5. Who can be a Christian model for me of patience? _____

_____

6. How can I develop this quality in my life? _____

_____

F. **A scripture verse I will memorize to help build patience into my life:** Eccles. 7:8; Rom. 5:3; 12:12; 1 Cor. 13:4, 7. _____

_____

G. **Self-evaluation:**

1. Am I able to accept unfavorable circumstances calmly?

2. Do I complain when plans do not go my way?

3. Is my life being lived out at a pace I can relax with, or do I always seem to be in a hurry and just a little behind?

4. Can I handle red lights, long lines, short delays, or do I quickly get angry or irritated?

5. Do I wait until I have enough money to buy something or am I constantly borrowing?

6. Am I more concerned for God's will to be done than my own desire to be fulfilled?

7. Am I easy to get along with when going through a difficult time or do people avoid me?

8. Do I relax when my plans have not worked out? Can I maintain self-control when situations change my plans?

9. Am I willing to go through trying times in order to develop patience?

10. Do I recognize obstacles as opportunities for God to build His character into me?

11. Have I thanked God for the lessons He has taught me through suffering?

Day 1: _____
_____
_____
_____
_____
_____
_____
_____
_____
_____
_____
_____
_____

Day 2: _____
_____
_____
_____
_____
_____
_____
_____
_____
_____
_____
_____
_____

Day 3: _____
_____
_____
_____
_____
_____
_____
_____
_____
_____
_____
_____
_____
_____

Words Of Wisdom: read a chapter from the Book of Proverbs corresponding with today's date (if today is the seventh, read chapter seven from the Book of Proverbs.)

Let your light so shine before men, that they may see your good works, and glorify your Father which is in heaven. Matthew 5:16

Day 4: _____

_____

_____

_____

_____

_____

_____

_____

_____

Day 5: _____

_____

_____

_____

_____

_____

_____

_____

_____

Day 6: _____

_____

_____

_____

_____

_____

_____

_____

_____

Day 7: _____

_____

_____

_____

_____

_____

_____

_____

_____

Prayer Needs/Requests & How God Responded: _____

_____

_____

_____

_____

_____

_____

_____

_____

_____

_____

_____

_____

_____

_____

Notes From This Week's Fellowship/Teaching: _____

_____

_____

_____

_____

_____

_____

_____

_____

_____

_____

_____

_____

_____

_____

_____

_____

_____

_____

_____

_____

_____

_____

_____

_____

Personal Accountability Checklist: (if in a group, have someone else check you)

☐ I completed the character or command promise study.
☐ I read a chapter from the Book Of Proverbs each day.
☐ I journaled each day.

Lesson 3: Courage

A. Definition of courage: _____

_____

B. An example from my everyday life: _____

_____

C. A positive example from the Bible: 1 Sam. 17:33-37; Dan. 3:16-18; 6:10-24; Acts 4:13-21. _____

_____

D. A negative example from the Bible: Num. 13:27-33; Matt. 26:69-74; John 19:12-16.

_____

E. Thinking about courage in my own life:

1. When have I clearly been courageous?_____

_____

2. In what situation did I fail to be courageous? _____

_____

3. What problem in my life could God use to build courage? _____

_____

4. Who can be a Christian model for me of courage? _____

_____

5. How can I develop this quality in my life?_____

_____

F. A scripture verse I will memorize to help build courage into my life: Josh. 1:9; Ps. 23:4; 27:1; Prov. 28:1; 29:25; Phil. 4:13; 2 Tim. 1:7; 1 John 4:18. _____

_____

G. Self-evaluation:

1. Does my courage depend only on my past success?
2. Do I often have to stand alone for what I believe?
3. Do my friends view me as courageous?
4. Do I look for opportunities to show courage?
5. Do I choose to be "one of the gang" when I should stand alone?
6. Have I avoided God-given opportunities because I lack courage?
7. Do others look to me for strength when danger threatens?
8. Am I confident that fears I now have will eventually be dealt with, or do I expect them to plague me the rest of my life?
9. Am I satisfied with who I am or do I envy people who are more courageous than I?
10. Have I been able to talk about my fears with someone close to me who can help me?
11. If people really knew me as I am, would they accept me?
12. Have I heard people I respect reveal the fears they have battled with?
13. Do I believe God has specific answers for the struggles I face?
14. Am I at the point where I am ready to trust God? (This may mean demonstrating the trust by seeking out help from a counselor).
15. Have I acquainted myself with examples of courage in the Bible so that my faith can be built through the Word of God?

Day 1: _____
_____
_____
_____
_____
_____
_____
_____
_____
_____
_____
_____
_____

Day 2: _____
_____
_____
_____
_____
_____
_____
_____
_____
_____
_____
_____
_____
_____

Day 3: _____
_____
_____
_____
_____
_____
_____
_____
_____
_____
_____
_____
_____
_____

 Words Of Wisdom: read a chapter from the Book of Proverbs corresponding with today's date (if today is the seventh, read chapter seven from the Book of Proverbs.)

If you love me, keep my commandments. John 14:15

Day 4: _____

_____

_____

_____

_____

_____

_____

_____

_____

_____

Day 5: _____

_____

_____

_____

_____

_____

_____

_____

_____

_____

Day 6: _____

_____

_____

_____

_____

_____

_____

_____

_____

_____

Day 7: _____

_____

_____

_____

_____

_____

_____

_____

_____

_____

Prayer Needs/Requests & How God Responded: _____

_____

_____

_____

_____

_____

_____

_____

_____

_____

_____

_____

_____

_____

Notes From This Week's Fellowship/Teaching: _____

_____

_____

_____

_____

_____

_____

_____

_____

_____

_____

_____

_____

_____

_____

_____

_____

_____

_____

_____

_____

_____

_____

_____

Personal Accountability Checklist: (if in a group, have someone else check you)

☐ I completed the character or command promise study.
☐ I read a chapter from the Book Of Proverbs each day.
☐ I journaled each day.

Lesson 4: Friendliness

A. Definition of friendliness: _____

_____

B. An example from my everyday life: _____

_____

C. **A positive example from the Bible:** Gen. 18:1-8; Luke 10:29-37; 10:38; 14:7-14.

_____

D. **A negative example from the Bible:** 1 Sam. 25:9-13; 2 Sam. 10:1-5; Luke 9:51-56; John 1:11; James 2:1-6. _____

_____

E. **Thinking about friendliness in my own life:**

1. When have I clearly been friendly? _____

_____

2. When, or to whom, have I failed to be friendly? _____

_____

3. Whom would God want me to be more friendly toward? _____

_____

4. Whom have I been friendly to that I should not have been? ____

_____

5. What problem in my life could God use to make me more friendly? _____

_____

6. How can I develop this quality in my life? _____

_____

F. **A scripture verse I will memorize to help build friendliness into my life:** Prov. 18:24; Luke 15:2; Rom. 12:13; Heb. 13:2; 1 Pet. 4:9. _____

_____

G. **Self-evaluation:**

1. Does my outward appearance indicate friendliness?
2. Do I enjoy being friendly?
3. Am I friendly out of love for others or for my own personal gain?
4. Does my friendliness depend on how friendly others are?
5. Am I friendly at all times or only when I feel "on top of the world"?
6. Am I honest enough to admit why I am not friendly in some circumstances?
7. When others in my group are unfriendly, do I prefer to conform, or can I be friendly on my own initiative?
8. Do I enjoy being part of a friendly group?
9. Have unpleasant encounters made me wary of strangers?
10. Does color, race, or creed restrict my friendliness?
11. Am I more friendly on "home territory" or can I be friendly away from home?
12. Do I have a desire to be friendly but feel inhibited?
13. Do I enjoy seeing people suffer when I am unfriendly?
14. Does God give me the right to be unfriendly toward certain people?
15. Do my moods radically affect my friendliness?
16. Am I cooperating with God to become a person who can be friendly to all people?

Day 1: _____
_____
_____
_____
_____
_____
_____
_____
_____
_____
_____
_____

Day 2: _____
_____
_____
_____
_____
_____
_____
_____
_____
_____
_____
_____
_____

Day 3: _____
_____
_____
_____
_____
_____
_____
_____
_____
_____
_____
_____
_____
_____
_____

 Words Of Wisdom: read a chapter from the Book of Proverbs corresponding with today's date (if today is the seventh, read chapter seven from the Book of Proverbs.)

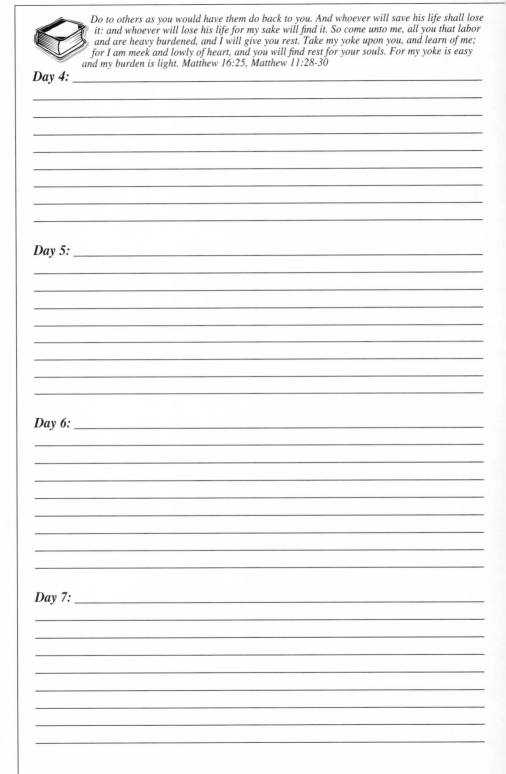

Do to others as you would have them do back to you. And whoever will save his life shall lose it: and whoever will lose his life for my sake will find it. So come unto me, all you that labor and are heavy burdened, and I will give you rest. Take my yoke upon you, and learn of me; for I am meek and lowly of heart, and you will find rest for your souls. For my yoke is easy and my burden is light. Matthew 16:25, Matthew 11:28-30

Day 4: _____
_____
_____
_____
_____
_____
_____
_____
_____

Day 5: _____
_____
_____
_____
_____
_____
_____
_____
_____

Day 6: _____
_____
_____
_____
_____
_____
_____
_____
_____

Day 7: _____
_____
_____
_____
_____
_____
_____
_____

Prayer Needs/Requests & How God Responded: _____

_____

_____

_____

_____

_____

_____

_____

_____

_____

_____

_____

_____

_____

_____

_____

_____

_____

Notes From This Week's Fellowship/Teaching: _____

_____

_____

_____

_____

_____

_____

_____

_____

_____

_____

_____

_____

_____

_____

_____

_____

_____

_____

_____

_____

_____

_____

_____

_____

_____

_____

_____

Personal Accountability Checklist: (if in a group, have someone else check you)
- ☐ I completed the character or command promise study.
- ☐ I read a chapter from the Book Of Proverbs each day.
- ☐ I journaled each day.

Lesson 5: Forgiveness

A. Definition of forgiveness: _____

_____

B. An example from my everyday life: _____

_____

C. **A positive example from the Bible:** Gen. 50:15-21; 1 Sam. 24:10-13; Luke 23:34; Acts 7:54-60. _____

D. **A negative example from the Bible:** Gen. 27:41-45; Jonah 3:10-4:2; Matt. 18:21-35.

_____

E. **Thinking about forgiveness in my own life:**

1. When have I been forgiving? _____

_____

2. When have I been unforgiving? _____

_____

3. What problem in my life could God use to make me more forgiving? _____

_____

4. Who can be a Christian model for me of forgiveness?_____

_____

5. How can I develop this quality in my life? _____

_____

F. **A scripture verse I will memorize to help build forgiveness into my life:** Prov. 19:11; Matt. 5:7; 6:12 or 14; Eph. 4:32. _____

_____

G. **Self-evaluation:**

1. Do I release those who offend me by telling God I forgive them?
2. Do I seek forgiveness from those I offend?
3. When I say, "I forgive you," or "That's all right," do I feel forgiveness in my heart or am I only mouthing the words?
4. Would I rather forgive than be forgiven?
5. When I ask God to forgive me, do I believe He does?
6. Do I carry the burden of an unforgiven sin?
7. Is there anyone I have refused to forgive?
8. Can Christians live full lives without forgiving?
9. Do forgiving people appear weak in today's society?
10. Has my attempt to forgive someone led to further conflict with that person?
11. Am I quick to ask for forgiveness or do I usually feel the other person needs to do so first?
12. Do I know anyone who seems able to forgive others regardless of what is done to him? Would I like to emulate that person?
13. Have I ever observed the destructive results of a person's unwillingness to forgive?
14. Can I name three people to whom I have said in the last six months, "Would you forgive me?"
15. Can I name three people whom I have forgiven during the last six months?

Day 1: _____

_____

_____

_____

_____

_____

_____

_____

_____

_____

_____

_____

Day 2: _____

_____

_____

_____

_____

_____

_____

_____

_____

_____

_____

_____

Day 3: _____

_____

_____

_____

_____

_____

_____

_____

_____

_____

_____

_____

_____

 Words Of Wisdom: read a chapter from the Book of Proverbs corresponding with today's date (if today is the seventh, read chapter seven from the Book of Proverbs.)

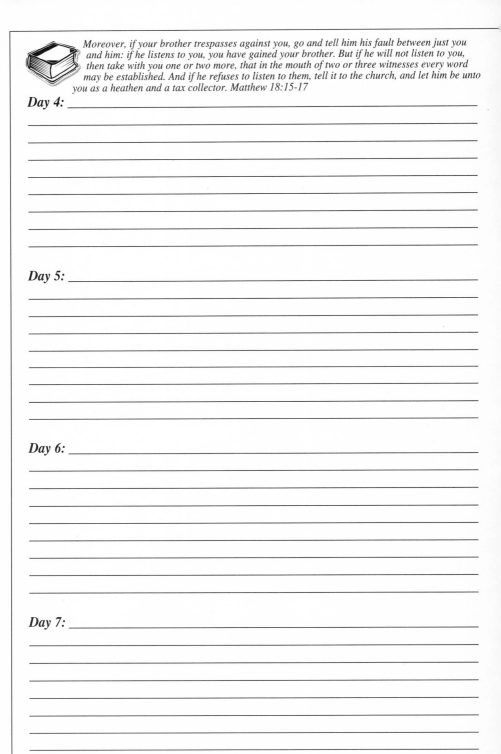

Moreover, if your brother trespasses against you, go and tell him his fault between just you and him: if he listens to you, you have gained your brother. But if he will not listen to you, then take with you one or two more, that in the mouth of two or three witnesses every word may be established. And if he refuses to listen to them, tell it to the church, and let him be unto you as a heathen and a tax collector. Matthew 18:15-17

Day 4: _____

_____
_____
_____
_____
_____
_____
_____
_____

Day 5: _____

_____
_____
_____
_____
_____
_____
_____
_____

Day 6: _____

_____
_____
_____
_____
_____
_____
_____
_____

Day 7: _____

_____
_____
_____
_____
_____
_____
_____
_____

Prayer Needs/Requests & How God Responded: _____

_____
_____
_____
_____
_____
_____
_____
_____
_____
_____
_____
_____
_____
_____

Notes From This Week's Fellowship/Teaching: _____

_____
_____
_____
_____
_____
_____
_____
_____
_____
_____
_____
_____
_____
_____
_____
_____
_____
_____
_____
_____
_____
_____
_____
_____
_____

Personal Accountability Checklist: (if in a group, have someone else check you)

- ☐ I completed the character or command promise study.
- ☐ I read a chapter from the Book Of Proverbs each day.
- ☐ I journaled each day.

Lesson 6: Honesty

A. Definition of honesty: _____

_____

B. An example from my everyday life: _____

_____

C. A positive example from the Bible: Gen. 31:36-42; 43:11, 12; Matt. 26:59-64. ___

_____

D. A negative example from the Bible: Gen. 26:9-11; 2 Sam. 11:1-27; Esther 7:1-10;
John 12:6; Acts 5:1-10. _____

_____

E. Thinking about honesty in my own life:

1. When have I been honest when it was not easy to do so? _____

_____

2. In what situation did I fail to be honest? _____

_____

3. What problem in my life could God use to build honesty? _____

_____

4. Who can be a Christian model for me of honesty? _____

_____

5. How can I develop this quality in my life? _____

_____

F. A scripture verse I will memorize to help build honesty into my life: Ps. 15:2; 19:14;
25:5; Prov. 21:6; John 14:6; 14:17; Eph. 4:15; Phil. 4:8. _____

_____

G. Self-evaluation:

1. Do people consider me an honest person?
2. Am I honest toward my parents/authorities?
3. Am I honest when I know I will be punished?
4. Am I honest when it may cost me popularity, a friend, a sense of security, a good grade?
5. Do I ever carry burdens because of dishonesty?
6. Do I mean what I say every time I make a statement?
7. Am I prone to exaggerate?
8. Do I enjoy freedom in my life because I am honest before God in all that I do?
9. Do dishonest people cause trouble in my life?
10. Do honest people bother me?
11. Is honesty a virtue I believe in, but not to the point of practicing it in all situations?
12. Do I demand honesty from others but not expect it from myself?
13. Most of us have been undercharged or have received too much change when making a purchase. Do I enjoy returning money in those situations?
14. Is it harder for me to be honest when I am alone? For instance, a boss wants eight hours of hard work. Do I try to get by with less when he is not around?
15. Have I rationalized dishonesty so that I don't feel as bad about it (e.g., calling an untruth a "white lie")?
16. Do I feel deep sorrow for the times I've been dishonest?
17. Is it more important for older people to be honest than young people? Do I have different standards for different ages?

Day 1: _____
_____
_____
_____
_____
_____
_____
_____
_____
_____
_____
_____
_____

Day 2: _____
_____
_____
_____
_____
_____
_____
_____
_____
_____
_____
_____
_____

Day 3: _____
_____
_____
_____
_____
_____
_____
_____
_____
_____
_____
_____
_____

 Words Of Wisdom: read a chapter from the Book of Proverbs corresponding with today's date (if today is the seventh, read chapter seven from the Book of Proverbs.)

When you have done all those things which are commanded of you, say, "We are unworthy servants, we have only done our duty." Luke 17:10

Day 4: _____
_____
_____
_____
_____
_____
_____
_____
_____

Day 5: _____
_____
_____
_____
_____
_____
_____
_____
_____
_____

Day 6: _____
_____
_____
_____
_____
_____
_____
_____
_____

Day 7: _____
_____
_____
_____
_____
_____
_____
_____
_____

Prayer Needs/Requests & How God Responded: _____

_____
_____
_____
_____
_____
_____
_____
_____
_____
_____
_____
_____
_____
_____
_____

Notes From This Week's Fellowship/Teaching: _____

_____
_____
_____
_____
_____
_____
_____
_____
_____
_____
_____
_____
_____
_____
_____
_____
_____
_____
_____
_____
_____
_____
_____
_____
_____

Personal Accountability Checklist: (if in a group, have someone else check you)

- ☐ I completed the character or command promise study.
- ☐ I read a chapter from the Book Of Proverbs each day.
- ☐ I journaled each day.

Lesson 7: Dependability

A. Definition of dependability: _____

_____

B. An example from my everyday life: _____

_____

C. **A positive example from the Bible:** Gen. 6:5-8; 7:1-5; Ruth 1:15-18; Matt. 24:42;
   25:13; Phil. 2:19-23. _____

   _____

D. **A negative example from the Bible:** 2 Sam. 3:26-30, 39; Matt. 25:21-30; 2 Tim. 4:9-
   11. _____

E. **Thinking about dependability in my own life:**

   1. When have I been dependable? _____

   _____

   2. In what situation did I fail to be dependable? _____

   _____

   3. What problem in my life could God use to make me more dependable? _____

   _____

   4. Who can be a Christian model for me of dependability? _____

   _____

   5. How can I develop this quality in my life? _____

   _____

F. **A scripture verse I will memorize to help build dependability into my life:** Prov.
   20:6; 28:20; Luke 16:10; 1 Cor. 4:2; Col. 3:22; Rev. 2:10. _____

   _____

G. **Self-evaluation:**
   1. Am I just as dependable when my teacher (or boss, parent, friend, pastor, etc.) is
      not around as when he/she is?
   2. Do I finish what I have started for someone else?
   3. Do I return things I borrow, or must the owners ask me for them?
   4. Do I refrain from talking about others, or do I gossip freely?
   5. Can people count on me to do a job if I promise I will?
   6. Do I loyally support those in authority over me?
   7. Do I adjust to the goals, desires and plans of those God puts over me, or do I
      resist until I get my way?
   8. Do I follow my Christian convictions even when I will face negative conse-
      quences?
   9. Do I ever take advantage of other people?
   10. Am I slow to believe a word of criticism about someone else or do I accept
       everything I hear?
   11. Do I give excuses when I have not been dependable? Do I rationalize why the job
       was not done or not done right?
   12. Am I faithful in attending meetings I am committed to? Do I come on time?
   13. Do people take me seriously when I say I plan to do something? Am I a person of
       my word?
   14. Can God count on me to follow through with assignments He gives me such as
       witnessing to a neighbor?

Day 1: _____
_____
_____
_____
_____

_____
_____
_____
_____
_____
_____
_____
_____

Day 2: _____
_____
_____
_____
_____
_____
_____
_____
_____
_____
_____
_____
_____

Day 3: _____
_____
_____
_____
_____
_____
_____
_____
_____
_____
_____
_____
_____

 Words Of Wisdom: read a chapter from the Book of Proverbs corresponding with today's date (if today is the seventh, read chapter seven from the Book of Proverbs.)

You have also heard it said, "Do not break your oaths, but perform them to the Lord". But I tell you, Swear not at all; neither by heaven; for it is God's throne: Nor by the earth; for it is his footstool: neither by Jerusalem; for it is the city of the great king. Neither swear by your head, because you cannot make one hair black or white. But let your communication be, yea, yea; nay, nay: for whatever is more than this comes from evil. Matthew 5:33-37

Day 4: _____
_____
_____
_____
_____
_____
_____
_____
_____

Day 5: _____
_____
_____
_____
_____
_____
_____
_____
_____

Day 6: _____
_____
_____
_____
_____
_____
_____
_____
_____

Day 7: _____
_____
_____
_____
_____
_____
_____
_____
_____

Prayer Needs/Requests & How God Responded: _____

_____

_____

_____

_____

_____

_____

_____

_____

_____

_____

_____

_____

_____

_____

Notes From This Week's Fellowship/Teaching: _____

_____

_____

_____

_____

_____

_____

_____

_____

_____

_____

_____

_____

_____

_____

_____

_____

_____

_____

_____

_____

_____

Personal Accountability Checklist: (if in a group, have someone else check you)
- ☐ I completed the character or command promise study.
- ☐ I read a chapter from the Book Of Proverbs each day.
- ☐ I journaled each day.

Lesson 8: Gratitude

A. Definition of gratitude: _____

_____

B. An example from my everyday life: _____

_____

C. A positive example from the Bible: 2 Sam. 2:5-7; Dan. 2:17-23; Rom. 16:1-12; Phil. 1:3-7. _____

_____

D. A negative example from the Bible: Gen. 31:36-42; Ex. 17:1-4; Luke 17:11-18. __

_____

E. Thinking about gratitude in my own life:

1. When have I shown gratitude in a specific way? _____

_____

2. In what situation did I fail to show gratitude? _____

_____

3. What problem in my life could God use to build gratitude? _____

_____

4. Who can be a Christian model for me of gratitude? _____

_____

5. How can I develop this quality in my life? _____

_____

F. A scripture verse I will memorize to help build gratitude into my life: Ps. 107:1; Phil. 4:6; Col. 3:17; 1 Thess. 5:18; Heb. 13:15. _____

_____

G. Self-evaluation:

1. Have I ever thanked my mother for all the trouble and effort she went through in bearing me and caring for me?
2. Have I ever thanked my mother for all the clothes she has washed, the meals she has cooked, the beds she has made, and the prayers she has prayed?
3. Do I regularly thank my mother and father for driving me to all my activities?
4. Have I ever thanked my father for supporting the family so well?
5. Is there a teacher who has meant a great deal to me, either recently or in years past? Have I thanked him/her?
6. Is there a friend who has been particularly good to me, at present or in the past? Have I said "thank you" for his/her kindness?
7. Is there someone who has helped me in my spiritual life, someone who challenged or encouraged me to get close to God? Have I thanked him or her?
8. Do I thank God for the blessings He brings to me...food, shelter, life, forgiveness, friends, a future, a free country, opportunity, challenges, work, health, etc.?
9. Am I able to thank God for difficult times that have taught me important lessons?
10. Would people who know me well consider me a thankful person, or would they say I tend to grumble, complain, criticize?
11. Is it easy for me to say, "I appreciate you"?
12. Can I think of anyone who might be resentful toward me because I forgot to say, "Thank you"?

Day 1: _____

_____

_____

_____

_____

_____

_____

_____

_____

_____

_____

_____

Day 2: _____

_____

_____

_____

_____

_____

_____

_____

_____

_____

_____

_____

_____

Day 3: _____

_____

_____

_____

_____

_____

_____

_____

_____

_____

_____

_____

_____

_____

 Words Of Wisdom: read a chapter from the Book of Proverbs corresponding with today's date (if today is the seventh, read chapter seven from the Book of Proverbs.)

Don't be called Rabbi for one is your Master, even Christ; and you are all brothers. And call no man on earth your father: for one is your Father, which is in heaven. Neither be called master, for one is your Master, even Christ. The greatest among you shall be called servant. Mth. 23:8-11

Day 4: _____

_____

_____

_____

_____

_____

_____

_____

Day 5: _____

_____

_____

_____

_____

_____

_____

_____

Day 6: _____

_____

_____

_____

_____

_____

_____

_____

Day 7: _____

_____

_____

_____

_____

_____

_____

_____

Prayer Needs/Requests & How God Responded: _____

_____
_____
_____
_____
_____
_____
_____
_____
_____
_____
_____
_____
_____

Notes From This Week's Fellowship/Teaching: _____

_____
_____
_____
_____
_____
_____
_____
_____
_____
_____
_____
_____
_____
_____
_____
_____
_____
_____
_____
_____
_____
_____
_____
_____
_____

Personal Accountability Checklist: (if in a group, have someone else check you)

☐ I completed the character or command promise study.
☐ I read a chapter from the Book Of Proverbs each day.
☐ I journaled each day.

Lesson 9: Self-Control

A. Definition of self-control: _____

_____

B. An example from my everyday life: _____

_____

C. **A positive example from the Bible:** Gen. 39:6-18; 2 Sam. 16:5-13; 1 Kings 19:9; Dan. 1:8-16. _____

D. **A negative example from the Bible:** Gen. 3:1-7; Num. 20:7-12; 2 Sam. 13:1-19; 1 Kings 21:1-7. _____

E. **Thinking about self-control in my own life:**

1. When have I shown self-control in a specific way? _____

_____

2. In what situation did I fail to show self-control? _____

_____

3. What problem in my life could God use to build self-control? _____

_____

4. Who can be a Christian model for me of self-control? _____

_____

5. How can I develop this quality in my life? _____

_____

F. **A scripture verse I will memorize to help build self-control into my life:** Prov. 16:32; 25:28; 1 Cor. 9:25; Gal. 5:16, 24; 1 Thess. 5:22; Titus 2:12. _____

_____

G. **Self-evaluation:**

1. Does my language always reflect self-control?
2. Do people find it difficult to make me upset?
3. What people have I wounded through careless words?
4. Do I control my appetite?
5. When I am tempted to compromise God's standards, do my convictions usually win out over my natural desires?
6. Has my self-control developed in the last year?
7. We are often encouraged to "tell it like it is." Do I know when it is wise and unwise to do so?
8. Would those of the opposite sex who know me well say I demonstrate self-control?
9. Our society tells us, "Enjoy yourself." Do I generally sacrifice moral standards to do that?
10. Am I happier when under restraint or when free to do as I please?
11. Have I made self-control a primary goal (although many consider it unimportant)?
12. Are God's limitations for my personal liberties worth obeying?
13. Can I agree with the statement: To be truly free is to be in control of my appetites and habits, not to be under their control?
14. Most of us have felt much guilt about areas in which we've lacked self-control. Am I presently carrying guilt for this reason?
15. Is it possible to gain victory over those areas that have defeated me?

Day 1: _____

_____

_____

_____

_____

_____

_____

_____

_____

_____

_____

_____

_____

_____

Day 2: _____

_____

_____

_____

_____

_____

_____

_____

_____

_____

_____

_____

_____

_____

Day 3: _____

_____

_____

_____

_____

_____

_____

_____

_____

_____

_____

_____

_____

Words Of Wisdom: read a chapter from the Book of Proverbs corresponding with today's date (if today is the seventh, read chapter seven from the Book of Proverbs.)

Then shall the King say to them on his right hand, Come, you blessed of my Father, inherit the kingdom prepared for you from the foundation of the world. For I was hungry and you gave me meat, I was thirsty, and you gave me a drink, I was a stranger, and you took me in, naked, and you clothed me, I was sick and you visited me, I was in prison and you came to me.
Matthew 25:34-36

Day 4: _____

_____
_____
_____
_____
_____
_____
_____
_____
_____

Day 5: _____

_____
_____
_____
_____
_____
_____
_____
_____
_____

Day 6: _____

_____
_____
_____
_____
_____
_____
_____
_____
_____

Day 7: _____

_____
_____
_____
_____
_____
_____
_____
_____
_____

Prayer Needs/Requests & How God Responded: _____

_____

_____

_____

_____

_____

_____

_____

_____

_____

_____

_____

_____

_____

_____

Notes From This Week's Fellowship/Teaching: _____

_____

_____

_____

_____

_____

_____

_____

_____

_____

_____

_____

_____

_____

_____

_____

_____

_____

_____

_____

_____

_____

_____

_____

_____

_____

_____

_____

Personal Accountability Checklist: (if in a group, have someone else check you)

- ☐ I completed the character or command promise study.
- ☐ I read a chapter from the Book Of Proverbs each day.
- ☐ I journaled each day.

Lesson 10: Humility

A. Definition of humility: _____

_____

B. An example from my everyday life: _____

_____

C. A positive example from the Bible: Luke 1:26-56; 7:1-10; John 1:19-28; 3:28-30; Phil. 2:3-11. _____

D. A negative example from the Bible: Isa. 14:12-17; Dan. 4:30-34; Luke 18:9-14. __

_____

E. Thinking about humility in my own life:

1. When have I been humble? _____

_____

2. When have I failed to be humble? _____

_____

3. What problem in my life could God use to build humility? _____

_____

4. Who can be a Christian model for me of humility? _____

_____

5. How can I develop this quality in my life? _____

_____

F. A scripture verse I will memorize to help build humility into my life: Ps. 138:6; Prov. 11:2; Matt. 5:3; 23:12; 1 Pet. 5:5, 6. _____

_____

G. Self-evaluation:

1. Do I quickly accept blame or do I tend to pass it on to others?

2. How often do I say, "Please forgive me; I was wrong"?

3. Am I a good listener, or do I shape my own comments while the other person talks?

4. Do I desire that others receive what is rightfully theirs – attention, glory, a special favor – or would I rather receive it?

5. Do I willingly accept tasks assigned to me?

6. Am I content with the gifts God has given me?

7. Do I accept God's judgments joyfully, as a means of learning true humility, or do I sulk when I get "spanked"?

8. Would those close to me consider me a humble person?

9. Do I accept jobs that are difficult for me because I want to learn to trust God, or do I pull back because I don't think I can do them?

10. Am I able to see my physical defects as marks of divine ownership?

11. Do I think a great deal about my reputation, my status in the group? Do I ever consider the reputation of Christ? Which is more important to me?

12. Do I freely give praise to others who deserve it?

13. Do I compliment others freely or am I always waiting for others to compliment me?

Day 1: _____
_____
_____
_____
_____
_____
_____
_____
_____
_____
_____
_____
_____

Day 2: _____
_____
_____
_____
_____
_____
_____
_____
_____
_____
_____
_____
_____

Day 3: _____
_____
_____
_____
_____
_____
_____
_____
_____
_____
_____
_____
_____

Words Of Wisdom: read a chapter from the Book of Proverbs corresponding with today's date (if today is the seventh, read chapter seven from the Book of Proverbs.)

Abide in me, and I in you. As the branch cannot bear fruit of itself, unless it abides in the vine, neither can you, unless you abide in me. I am the vine, you are the branches: He that abides in me, and I in him, brings forth much fruit: for without me you can do nothing. John 15:4-5

Day 4: _____

_____

_____

_____

_____

_____

_____

_____

_____

Day 5: _____

_____

_____

_____

_____

_____

_____

_____

_____

Day 6: _____

_____

_____

_____

_____

_____

_____

_____

_____

Day 7: _____

_____

_____

_____

_____

_____

_____

_____

_____

Prayer Needs/Requests & How God Responded: _____

_____
_____
_____
_____
_____
_____
_____
_____
_____
_____
_____
_____
_____
_____

Notes From This Week's Fellowship/Teaching: _____

_____
_____
_____
_____
_____
_____
_____
_____
_____
_____
_____
_____
_____
_____
_____
_____
_____
_____
_____
_____
_____
_____
_____
_____
_____

Personal Accountability Checklist: (if in a group, have someone else check you)
- ☐ I completed the character or command promise study.
- ☐ I read a chapter from the Book Of Proverbs each day.
- ☐ I journaled each day.

Lesson 11: Responsibility

A. Definition of responsibility: _____

_____

B. An example from my everyday life: _____

_____

C. **A positive example from the Bible:** Gen. 41:37-45; Ruth 1:11-13; Esther 4:13-17; Matt. 25:14-23. _____

D. **A negative example from the Bible:** Gen. 3:8-13; 4:8-10; 25:29-34; Ex. 32:21-24; Matt. 27:24, 25. _____

E. **Thinking about responsibility in my own life:**

1. When have I been responsible? _____

_____

2. When have I failed to be responsible? _____

_____

3. What problem in my life could God use to build responsibility? _____

_____

4. Who can be a Christian model for me of responsibility? _____

_____

5. How can I develop this quality in my life? _____

_____

F. **A scripture verse I will memorize to help build responsibility into my life:** Gal. 6:5; 1 Pet. 4:10. _____

_____

G. **Self-evaluation:**

1. Do I accept responsibility for my actions at all times?
2. Do I accept responsibility for my failures, or do I tend to make excuses?
3. Do I enjoy being responsible for other people's actions?
4. When I have not acted responsibly, do I feel angry toward myself?
5. When I look at my responsibilities, do I tend to worry?
6. Do I think more about my responsibilities than about my rights?
7. Do I take care of other people's property as I would my own?
8. Is being "my brother's keeper" more important than my freedom of speech?
9. Do people in authority entrust me with extra responsibilities?
10. Do I seek additional responsibility or do I avoid it?
11. Am I responsible to keep scheduled appointments and to be on time?
12. Do I carry out my jobs properly when my superiors are not present?
13. Do I avoid making rash promises?
14. Do I keep promises I make?
15. Am I cooperating with God to make myself more responsible?

Day 1: _____
_____
_____
_____
_____
_____
_____
_____
_____
_____
_____
_____
_____

Day 2: _____
_____
_____
_____
_____
_____
_____
_____
_____
_____
_____
_____
_____

Day 3: _____
_____
_____
_____
_____
_____
_____
_____
_____
_____
_____
_____
_____

 Words Of Wisdom: read a chapter from the Book of Proverbs corresponding with today's date (if today is the seventh, read chapter seven from the Book of Proverbs.)

Judge not, and you will not be judged: condemn not, and you will not be condemned: Forgive and you will be forgiven: Give and it will be given to you; good measure, pressed down, shaken together and running over will men give into your bosom. For with the same measure that you measure out, it will be measured to you again. Luke 6:37-38

Day 4: _____

_____
_____
_____
_____
_____
_____
_____
_____

Day 5: _____

_____
_____
_____
_____
_____
_____
_____
_____

Day 6: _____

_____
_____
_____
_____
_____
_____
_____
_____

Day 7: _____

_____
_____
_____
_____
_____
_____
_____
_____

Prayer Needs/Requests & How God Responded: _____

_____
_____
_____
_____
_____
_____
_____
_____
_____
_____
_____
_____
_____
_____

Notes From This Week's Fellowship/Teaching: _____

_____
_____
_____
_____
_____
_____
_____
_____
_____
_____
_____
_____
_____
_____
_____
_____
_____
_____
_____
_____
_____
_____
_____
_____
_____

Personal Accountability Checklist: (if in a group, have someone else check you)
- ☐ I completed the character or command promise study.
- ☐ I read a chapter from the Book Of Proverbs each day.
- ☐ I journaled each day.

Lesson 12: Contentment

A. Are you basically a contented person? Instead of answering with a yes or no, respond by writing several sentences about yourself. Before writing, ask yourself, "Am I satisfied with life – with myself, my family, my future, my gifts? Or am I discontented?": _____

_____

_____

_____

B. Explain (in four sentences or more) why you feel you are, or are not, a contented person: _____

_____

_____

_____

C. Are you developing in contentment? Explain: _____

_____

_____

_____

D. Study the following passages. What do they teach you about contentment? Num. 11:1-15; Rom 9:19-21; Phil. 4:10-13; 1 Tim. 6:6-9. _____

_____

_____

_____

E. Give a definition of contentment: _____

_____

_____

_____

F. Who is the most contented person you know? Memorize Phil. 4:11: "Not that I complain of want; for I have learned, in whatever state I am, to be content."

G. Self-evaluation:
   1. Do I expect to be contented regardless of what happens to me?
   2. Do I experience contentment in disturbing situations?
   3. Am I contented only when things go "my way"?
   4. Is my contentment contagious?
   5. Do I view contented people as being lazy?
   6. Are Christians the only contented people in our world?
   7. Does my present life-style encourage contentment?
   8. Would I have to change my life-style to become a contented person?
   9. Am I willing to change my life-style in order to experience contentment?
   10. If I am not contented, do I know why I am not?
   11. Do I envy people who have more possessions than I?
   12. Do I have enough (of whatever it takes) to be content?
   13. Do I ever feel resentment toward God for holding back some of His blessings from me?
   14. Do I believe God is a Father who loves to give me good gifts, or do I believe God is stingy and overbearing?
   15. Am I cooperating with God to bring me to the place where I will be able to say, "I have learned in whatever state I am to be content"?

Day 1: _____

_____

_____

_____

_____

_____

_____

_____

_____

_____

_____

Day 2: _____

_____

_____

_____

_____

_____

_____

_____

_____

_____

_____

Day 3: _____

_____

_____

_____

_____

_____

_____

_____

_____

_____

_____

Words Of Wisdom: read a chapter from the Book of Proverbs corresponding with today's date (if today is the seventh, read chapter seven from the Book of Proverbs.)

He that receives a prophet in the name of a prophet will receive a prophet's reward; and he that receives a righteous man in the name of a righteous man will receive a righteous man's reward. And whoever gives a cold drink of water to one of these little ones only in the name of a disciple, truly I tell you, he will in no way, lose his reward. Matthew 10:41-42

Day 4: _____

_____

_____

_____

_____

_____

_____

_____

_____

_____

Day 5: _____

_____

_____

_____

_____

_____

_____

_____

_____

_____

Day 6: _____

_____

_____

_____

_____

_____

_____

_____

_____

_____

Day 7: _____

_____

_____

_____

_____

_____

_____

_____

_____

_____

Prayer Needs/Requests & How God Responded: _____

_____

_____

_____

_____

_____

_____

_____

_____

_____

_____

_____

_____

_____

_____

_____

Notes From This Week's Fellowship/Teaching: _____

_____

_____

_____

_____

_____

_____

_____

_____

_____

_____

_____

_____

_____

_____

_____

_____

_____

_____

_____

_____

_____

_____

_____

_____

_____

_____

_____

_____

_____

_____

Personal Accountability Checklist: (if in a group, have someone else check you)
- ☐ I completed the character or command promise study.
- ☐ I read a chapter from the Book Of Proverbs each day.
- ☐ I journaled each day.

Lesson 13: Gentleness

A. Definition of gentleness: _____

_____

B. An example from my everyday life: _____

_____

C. **A positive example from the Bible:** Isa. 40:11; 42:1-3; Matt. 11:28-29; Luke 7:36-50; 10:38-42; John 8:1-11; 1 Thess. 2:7-8. _____

_____

D. **A negative example from the Bible:** Num. 20:2-13; 2 Sam. 18:10-15; 19:1-8; 1 Kings 21:5-14; Luke 9:51-56. _____

_____

E. **Thinking about gentleness in my own life:**

1. When have I been gentle? _____

_____

2. In what situation did I fail to be gentle? _____

_____

3. What problem in my life could God use to build gentleness? _____

_____

4. Who can be a Christian model for me of gentleness? _____

_____

5. How can I develop this quality in my life? _____

_____

F. **A scripture verse I will memorize to help build gentleness into my life:** Ps. 25:9; 37:11; Matt. 5:5; 11:29; James 3:17. _____

_____

G. **Self-evaluation:**

1. Do I associate gentleness with weakness?

2. Are females more gentle than males?

3. Do I enjoy being with small children?

4. Am I comfortable with the elderly?

5. If I am gentle, will I be accepted in my peer group?

6. Do gentle people attract me?

7. Do I avoid harsh and abusive people?

8. Do I become more gentle when I spend time worshiping Jesus?

9. Do I excuse myself when I am harsh or unkind?

10. Is the ability to stifle true emotion a character strength?

11. Do I harden my heart?

Day 1: _____
_____
_____
_____
_____
_____
_____
_____
_____
_____
_____
_____
_____

Day 2: _____
_____
_____
_____
_____
_____
_____
_____
_____
_____
_____
_____
_____

Day 3: _____
_____
_____
_____
_____
_____
_____
_____
_____
_____
_____
_____
_____

Words Of Wisdom: read a chapter from the Book of Proverbs corresponding with today's date (if today is the seventh, read chapter seven from the Book of Proverbs.)

There is no man that has left house, or brothers, or sisters, or father, or mother, or wife, or children, or lands, for my sake, and the gospels', but he will receive a hundredfold now in this time, houses, and brothers, and sisters, and mothers, and children, and lands, with persecutions; and in the world to come, eternal life. Mark 10:29-30

Day 4: _____

_____

_____

_____

_____

_____

_____

_____

_____

Day 5: _____

_____

_____

_____

_____

_____

_____

_____

_____

Day 6: _____

_____

_____

_____

_____

_____

_____

_____

_____

Day 7: _____

_____

_____

_____

_____

_____

_____

_____

_____

***Prayer Needs/Requests & How God Responded:**_____

_____

_____

_____

_____

_____

_____

_____

_____

_____

_____

_____

_____

_____

_____

_____

_____

_____

*Notes From This Week's Fellowship/Teaching:*_____

_____

_____

_____

_____

_____

_____

_____

_____

_____

_____

_____

_____

_____

_____

_____

_____

_____

_____

_____

_____

_____

_____

_____

_____

_____

_____

Personal Accountability Checklist: (if in a group, have someone else check you)
- ☐ I completed the character or command promise study.
- ☐ I read a chapter from the Book Of Proverbs each day.
- ☐ I journaled each day.

Lesson 14: Generosity

A. Definition of generosity: _____

_____

B. An example from my everyday life: _____

_____

C. **A positive example from the Bible:** Ex. 36:2-7; Luke 7:44; 8:3; 10:33-37; 21:1-4; 2 Cor. 8:1-7. _____

D. **A negative example from the Bible:** Hag. 1:2-9; Mal. 3:8-12; Matt. 25:31-46; 26:6-13.

_____

E. **Thinking about generosity in my own life:**

1. When have I been generous? _____

_____

2. In what situation did I fail to be generous? _____

_____

3. What problem in my life could God use to build generosity? _____

_____

4. Who can be a Christian model for me of generosity? _____

_____

5. How can I develop this quality in my life? _____

F. **A scripture verse I will memorize to help build generosity into my life:** Ps. 41:1; Prov. 11:24, 25; 13:7; 19:6; 28:27; Eccles. 11:1; Luke 6:38; 12:34; 2 Cor. 9:6. ____

_____

G. **Self-evaluation:**

1. Do I enjoy giving away things that are precious to me?
2. Do I like to surprise people with special gifts?
3. Do the material needs of others move me to give sacrificially?
4. Has tithing become a spiritual adventure for me?
5. Am I supposed to wait until I am a certain age before I start giving consistently to the work of the Lord?
6. Do I know anyone who has a special gift of giving? Have I noticed if he is a happy person?
7. Would those who know me well consider me a generous person?
8. Am I hospitable? Do I enjoy making people feel at home in my house and treating them as honored guests?
9. Am I as generous with time as I am with money?
10. Do I know what motivates me to be generous?
11. Am I more generous to friends than to family members?
12. Do I wait for someone else to offer to pay the check when a group of us eat out together?
13. Am I generous with a tip when it is appropriate?
14. Are there areas in which I am especially selfish?
15. Am I generous to people that do not appeal to me?
16. Do I want to become more generous with my time, money, and possessions?

Day 1: _____

_____

_____

_____

_____

_____

_____

_____

_____

_____

_____

Day 2: _____

_____

_____

_____

_____

_____

_____

_____

_____

_____

_____

Day 3: _____

_____

_____

_____

_____

_____

_____

_____

_____

_____

_____

 Words Of Wisdom: read a chapter from the Book of Proverbs corresponding with today's date (if today is the seventh, read chapter seven from the Book of Proverbs.)

Know this, that if the owner of the house had known when the thief would come, he would have watched and not allowed his house to be broken up. Therefore, you also, should be ready, for at a time that you think not, the Son of man will come. Matthew 24:43-44

Day 4: _____
_____
_____
_____
_____
_____
_____
_____
_____
_____

Day 5: _____
_____
_____
_____
_____
_____
_____
_____
_____

Day 6: _____
_____
_____
_____
_____
_____
_____
_____
_____

Day 7: _____
_____
_____
_____
_____
_____
_____
_____
_____

Prayer Needs/Requests & How God Responded: _____

_____
_____
_____
_____
_____
_____
_____
_____
_____
_____
_____
_____
_____

Notes From This Week's Fellowship/Teaching: _____

_____
_____
_____
_____
_____
_____
_____
_____
_____
_____
_____
_____
_____
_____
_____
_____
_____
_____
_____
_____
_____
_____
_____
_____
_____

Personal Accountability Checklist: (if in a group, have someone else check you)

☐ I completed the character or command promise study.
☐ I read a chapter from the Book Of Proverbs each day.
☐ I journaled each day.

Lesson 15: Purity

A. Definition of purity: _____

_____

B. An example from my everyday life: _____

_____

C. **A positive example from the Bible:** Gen. 39:6-18; Luke 1:26-37; John 8:34-47; 1 Cor. 13. _____

_____

D. **A negative example from the Bible:** Judg. 16:1-6, 15-17; 2 Sam. 11:1-27; 13:1-14; Matt. 14:1-12. _____

E. **Thinking about generosity in my own life:**

1. When have I shown strength in the area of purity? _____

_____

2. How have I shown weakness in this area? _____

_____

3. What problem in my life could God use to make me pure in thought, word and deed?

_____

4. Who can be a Christian model for me of purity? _____

_____

5. How can I develop this quality in my life? _____

_____

F. **A scripture verse I will memorize to help build purity into my life:** Matt. 5:8; Phil. 4:8; 1 Tim. 1:5, 5:22; James 4:8. _____

_____

G. **Self-evaluation:**

1. Do I strive to keep myself holy "as my Heavenly Father is holy"?
2. Do I sacrifice popularity to maintain my purity?
3. Am I willing to reject immoral thoughts, etc., so that I can present a pure body, soul and spirit to God?
4. Thinking about pure water: am I an iceberg, a clear mountain stream, a muddy creek, or a stagnant mire?
5. Do my thoughts ever become clouded with smutty jokes or immoral fantasies?
6. Do I have a friend to whom I can confess problems of impurity?
7. Do I consider myself guilty of impure actions even if no one sees me?
8. Does God expect me to be a pure as He expected people to be in Bible times?
9. Do I use God's standard for purity?
10. Have I changed any doctrinal positions because of moral problems?
11. Does the thought of being pure sound attractive or prudish to me?
12. Are my friends committed to holy living?
13. Do I want to marry someone with high moral standards?
14. Do I want to be a marriage partner with high moral standards?
15. Am I convinced that personal purity is possible in our society?
16. Can God forgive all my impurity?
17. Am I cooperating with God to make myself "pure in heart"?

Day 1: _____
_____
_____
_____
_____

_____
_____
_____
_____
_____
_____
_____
_____

Day 2: _____
_____
_____
_____
_____
_____
_____
_____
_____
_____
_____
_____
_____

Day 3: _____
_____
_____
_____
_____
_____
_____
_____
_____
_____
_____
_____
_____
_____

 Words Of Wisdom: read a chapter from the Book of Proverbs corresponding with today's date (if today is the seventh, read chapter seven from the Book of Proverbs.)

Whoever does not bear his cross, and come after me, forsaking all that he has, cannot be my disciple. Luke 14:27, 33

Day 4: _____
_____
_____
_____
_____
_____
_____
_____
_____
_____

Day 5: _____
_____
_____
_____
_____
_____
_____
_____
_____
_____
_____

Day 6: _____
_____
_____
_____
_____
_____
_____
_____
_____
_____
_____

Day 7: _____
_____
_____
_____
_____
_____
_____
_____
_____
_____

Prayer Needs/Requests & How God Responded: _____

_____
_____
_____
_____
_____
_____
_____
_____
_____
_____
_____
_____
_____

Notes From This Week's Fellowship/Teaching: _____

_____
_____
_____
_____
_____
_____
_____
_____
_____
_____
_____
_____
_____
_____
_____
_____
_____
_____
_____
_____
_____
_____
_____
_____
_____

Personal Accountability Checklist: (if in a group, have someone else check you)
- ☐ I completed the character or command promise study.
- ☐ I read a chapter from the Book Of Proverbs each day.
- ☐ I journaled each day.

Lesson 16: Confidence

A. Definition of confidence: _____

_____

B. An example from my everyday life: _____

_____

C. **A positive example from the Bible:** 1 Sam. 14:6-15; 1 Kings 17:1; 18:17-19; Ps. 27; Dan. 6:19-23; Acts 27:21-26. _____

_____

D. **A negative example from the Bible:** Gen. 3:8-13; 20:8-12; 1 Sam. 28:3-7; Mark 6:14-29. _____

_____

E. **Thinking about confidence in my own life:**

1. When have I been confident? _____

_____

2. In what situation did I fail to be confident? _____

_____

3. What problem in my life could God use to build confidence? _____

_____

4. Who can be a Christian model for me of confidence? _____

_____

5. How can I develop this quality in my life? _____

_____

F. **A scripture verse I will memorize to help build confidence into my life:** Prov. 3:25-26; 14:26; Heb. 4:16; 10:35; Phil. 4:13; 1 John 3:21; 5:14. _____

_____

G. **Self-evaluation:**

1. Whom do I know that is confident because he knows how to trust God?
2. Whom do I know that is confident because he is naturally gifted in a certain area?
3. In what areas am I confident?
4. What is the basis of my confidence?
5. Am I basically a fearful or confident person?
6. When do I most lack confidence?
7. Is there a relationship in my life between sin and loss of confidence?
8. Do I build up people's confidence in themselves?
9. Do I desire to be a confidence builder?
10. Has my home been a place where my confidence has been built?
11. What kind of fears do I allow to control me?
12. Do my friends build me up in a positive way?
13. Can I name four people who love me no matter what I do?
14. Do I habitually tear myself down?
15. Do people who are more confident than I make me jealous?
16. Am I cooperating with God to make me a confident person?

Day 1: _____
_____
_____
_____
_____
_____
_____
_____
_____
_____
_____
_____
_____

Day 2: _____
_____
_____
_____
_____
_____
_____
_____
_____
_____
_____
_____
_____

Day 3: _____
_____
_____
_____
_____
_____
_____
_____
_____
_____
_____
_____
_____

Words Of Wisdom: read a chapter from the Book of Proverbs corresponding with today's date (if today is the seventh, read chapter seven from the Book of Proverbs.)

Go therefore, and teach all nations, to obey all things that I have commanded you; and, lo, I am with you always, even unto the end of the world. Amen. Matthew 28:19-20

Day 4: _____

_____
_____
_____
_____
_____
_____
_____

Day 5: _____

_____
_____
_____
_____
_____
_____
_____

Day 6: _____

_____
_____
_____
_____
_____
_____
_____

Day 7: _____

_____
_____
_____
_____
_____
_____
_____

Prayer Needs/Requests & How God Responded: _____

_____

_____

_____

_____

_____

_____

_____

_____

_____

_____

_____

_____

_____

_____

Notes From This Week's Fellowship/Teaching: _____

_____

_____

_____

_____

_____

_____

_____

_____

_____

_____

_____

_____

_____

_____

_____

_____

_____

_____

_____

_____

_____

_____

_____

_____

Personal Accountability Checklist: (if in a group, have someone else check you)

- ☐ I completed the character or command promise study.
- ☐ I read a chapter from the Book Of Proverbs each day.
- ☐ I journaled each day.

Lesson 17: Encouragement

A. Definition of encouragement: _____

_____

B. An example from my everyday life: _____

_____

C. A positive example from the Bible: Neh. 2:17-20; 1 Sam. 23:15-18; Matt. 3:16, 17; 26:6-13; Luke 3:21, 22; Phil. 1:3-11. _____

_____

D. A negative example from the Bible: Num. 13:25-33; 1 Kings 12:20; Luke 15:25-32.

_____

E. Thinking about encouragement in my own life:

 1. When have I given encouragement to someone? _____

_____

 2. When have I especially needed encouragement? _____

_____

 3. What problem in my life could God use to make me an "encourager"? _____

_____

 4. Who can be a Christian model for me of encouragement? _____

_____

 5. How can I develop this quality in my life? _____

_____

F. A scripture verse I will memorize to help build encouragement into my life: Ps. 143:3; Matt. 3:17; John 14:1; 1 Thess. 5:11; 5:14; Heb. 3:13; 10:24. _____

_____

G. Self-evaluation:

 1. Do my words of encouragement easily outweigh words of correction or criticism?
 2. Do people become more cheerful around me?
 3. Would my family consider me an encouraging person?
 4. Is it easy for me to praise others?
 5. Am I careful to ask forgiveness of others when I have given a negative report or discouraging word?
 6. Have I been diligent to encourage those I associate with – children, students, employees, husband/wife, brothers, sisters, fellow church members?
 7. Have I been diligent to encourage those God has placed over me – teachers, employers, elders, ministers, church leaders, civil servants, government leaders?
 8. Do I pass along only good news and swallow gossip, or do I delight in sharing bad news?
 9. Does my conversation with friends generally build people up?
 10. Do I think more about giving praise than receiving it?
 11. Do I desire to become an "encourager"?
 12. Am I able to encourage those who have hurt me? Can I "bless those who persecute" me as Jesus commands?
 13. Have I recognized how encouraging God is to His whole creation? To me?
 14. Do patient people bother me?
 15. Do I avoid jobs that will test my patience?
 16. Has my impatience caused me to be unpopular?
 17. Am I patient enough in my personal prayer time so that God has a chance to communicate with me?

Day 1: _____

_____

_____

_____

_____

_____

_____

_____

_____

_____

_____

_____

Day 2: _____

_____

_____

_____

_____

_____

_____

_____

_____

_____

_____

_____

_____

Day 3: _____

_____

_____

_____

_____

_____

_____

_____

_____

_____

_____

_____

_____

Words Of Wisdom: read a chapter from the Book of Proverbs corresponding with today's date (if today is the seventh, read chapter seven from the Book of Proverbs.)

Yes if any man serve me, let him follow me, and where I am, there will my servant be: if any man serve me, him will my Father honor. John 12:26

Day 4: _____

_____
_____
_____
_____
_____
_____
_____
_____

Day 5: _____

_____
_____
_____
_____
_____
_____
_____
_____

Day 6: _____

_____
_____
_____
_____
_____
_____
_____
_____

Day 7: _____

_____
_____
_____
_____
_____
_____
_____
_____

Prayer Needs/Requests & How God Responded: _____

_____

_____

_____

_____

_____

_____

_____

_____

_____

_____

_____

_____

_____

_____

_____

_____

_____

Notes From This Week's Fellowship/Teaching: _____

_____

_____

_____

_____

_____

_____

_____

_____

_____

_____

_____

_____

_____

_____

_____

_____

_____

_____

_____

_____

_____

_____

_____

_____

Personal Accountability Checklist: (if in a group, have someone else check you)

- ☐ I completed the character or command promise study.
- ☐ I read a chapter from the Book Of Proverbs each day.
- ☐ I journaled each day.

Lesson 18: Availability

A. Definition of availability: _____
_____

B. An example from my everyday life: _____
_____

C. **A positive example from the Bible:** Gen. 12:1-9; Matt. 4:18-22; Luke 1:26-38; 18:15-16; Acts 6:1-8. _____

D. **A negative example from the Bible:** Gen. 3:9-10; Ex. 4:1-17; Jonah 1:1-4: Matt. 25:14-30; 2 Tim. 4:9, 10. _____

E. **Thinking about availability in my own life:**

1. When have I been most available to the Lord or others? _____
_____

2. In what situation did I fail to be available? _____
_____

3. What problem in my life could God use to build availability? _____
_____

4. Who can be a Christian model for me of availability? _____
_____

5. How can I develop this quality in my life? _____
_____

F. **A scripture verse I will memorize to help build availability into my life:** Isa. 6:8; Luke 1:38; 16:10; Rom. 6:13; 12:1, 6; 1 Cor. 4:2. _____
_____

G. **Self-evaluation:**

1. Have I shown to my parents, friends, associates that I am available to them?
2. Do people often call on me for help?
3. Am I using my gifts to build up the body of Christ?
4. Have I arranged my priorities so that I am able to say "yes" to legitimate needs?
5. Am I free from the tyranny of time so that I don't have to keep telling everyone how busy I am?
6. Do I willingly accept assignments given to me?
7. Am I willing to say "yes" to jobs that are beyond me, knowing that God will give me grace?
8. Do I spend time listening to God so that I am sensitive to what He wants me to do?
9. Am I able to view interruptions as opportunities to meet needs, or do I allow them to frustrate me?
10. Have I relinquished my own goals so that I can pursue God's?
11. Have I said to God, as Isaiah did, "Here am I, send me"?
12. Has God won the battle in my life over whose will is going to reign, God's or mine?
13. Have I dealt with the guilt of not being available for someone when I knew God wanted me to be?
14. Am I satisfied with my present level of availability to God and to others?

Day 1: _____
_____
_____
_____
_____
_____
_____
_____
_____
_____
_____
_____
_____

Day 2: _____
_____
_____
_____
_____
_____
_____
_____
_____
_____
_____
_____
_____
_____

Day 3: _____
_____
_____
_____
_____
_____
_____
_____
_____
_____
_____
_____
_____
_____
_____

Words Of Wisdom: read a chapter from the Book of Proverbs corresponding with today's date (if today is the seventh, read chapter seven from the Book of Proverbs.)

And when you make a feast, call the poor, the maimed, the lame and the blind, and you will be blessed; for they cannot repay you; and you will be repaid at the resurrection of the just.
Luke 14:13-14

Day 4: _____
_____
_____
_____
_____
_____
_____
_____
_____
_____

Day 5: _____
_____
_____
_____
_____
_____
_____
_____
_____
_____

Day 6: _____
_____
_____
_____
_____
_____
_____
_____
_____

Day 7: _____
_____
_____
_____
_____
_____
_____
_____
_____

Prayer Needs/Requests & How God Responded: _____

_____
_____
_____
_____
_____
_____
_____
_____
_____
_____
_____
_____
_____
_____

Notes From This Week's Fellowship/Teaching: _____

_____
_____
_____
_____
_____
_____
_____
_____
_____
_____
_____
_____
_____
_____
_____
_____
_____
_____
_____
_____
_____
_____
_____
_____
_____
_____

Personal Accountability Checklist: (if in a group, have someone else check you)
- [ ] I completed the character or command promise study.
- [ ] I read a chapter from the Book Of Proverbs each day.
- [ ] I journaled each day.

Lesson 19: Attentiveness

A. Definition of attentiveness: _____

_____

B. An example from my everyday life: _____

_____

C. A positive example from the Bible: Ex. 18:19-24; Ps. 34; John 10:1-5; Rev. 3:15-22.

_____

D. A negative example from the Bible: Num. 22:15-35; Prov. 29:12; Isa. 7:10-15; Matt. 13:10-17; 16:21-25; John 6:58-61. _____

E. Thinking about attentiveness in my own life:

1. When have I been attentive? _____

_____

2. In what situation did I fail to be attentive? _____

_____

3. To whom would God want me to be more attentive?_____

_____

4. What problem in my life could God use to build attentiveness? _____

_____

5. How can I develop this quality in my life? _____

_____

F. A scripture verse I will memorize to help build attentiveness into my life: Ps. 25:5; 40:1; Prov. 12:15; 23:12; 23:22; Mark 4:23; Heb. 2:1. _____

_____

G. Self-evaluation:

1. Would those close to me consider me to be a good listener?
2. Am I a good listener? Do my facial expressions and other gestures show that I am listening intently?
3. When I am spoken to, do I stop what I am doing, look and listen?
4. Do I always look at the person who is speaking to me or do I glance away to other people or other distractions?
5. Are there certain people I pay more attention to than others? Do I know why?
6. How hard do my parents have to work to gain my attention?
7. Do I listen to another person without wishing he would stop so that I could say something more interesting?
8. Do I listen carefully when assignments are given to me so that the information is clear?
9. Do I ever make others uncomfortable by looking at my watch when they are talking?
10. Have I cultivated the practice of responding to the inner voice of the Holy Spirit?
11. Do my personal prayer times include times of quiet meditation and listening to God?
12. Have I told God that I will do whatever He tells me to do if He makes it clear to me?
13. Do I have a recent testimony of how Scripture has spoken to me?

Day 1: _____
_____
_____
_____
_____
_____
_____
_____
_____
_____
_____
_____
_____

Day 2: _____
_____
_____
_____
_____
_____
_____
_____
_____
_____
_____
_____
_____

Day 3: _____
_____
_____
_____
_____
_____
_____
_____
_____
_____
_____
_____
_____
_____

Words Of Wisdom: read a chapter from the Book of Proverbs corresponding with today's date (if today is the seventh, read chapter seven from the Book of Proverbs.)

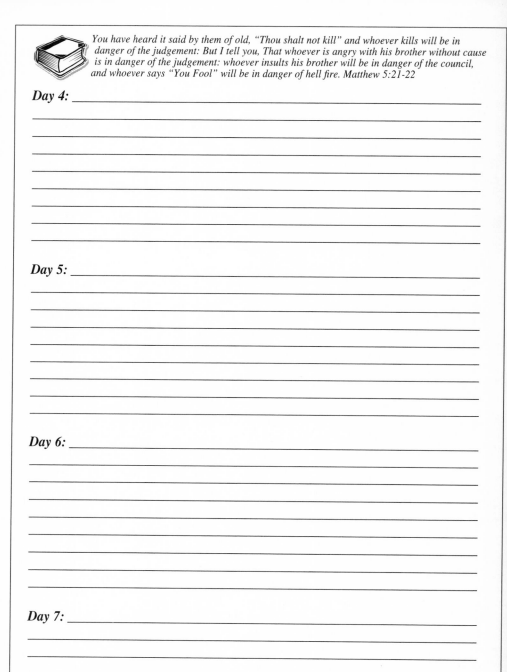

You have heard it said by them of old, "Thou shalt not kill" and whoever kills will be in danger of the judgement: But I tell you, That whoever is angry with his brother without cause is in danger of the judgement: whoever insults his brother will be in danger of the council, and whoever says "You Fool" will be in danger of hell fire. Matthew 5:21-22

Day 4: _____

_____
_____
_____
_____
_____
_____
_____
_____

Day 5: _____

_____
_____
_____
_____
_____
_____
_____
_____
_____

Day 6: _____

_____
_____
_____
_____
_____
_____
_____
_____

Day 7: _____

_____
_____
_____
_____
_____
_____
_____
_____

Prayer Needs/Requests & How God Responded: _____

_____
_____
_____
_____
_____
_____
_____
_____
_____
_____
_____
_____
_____
_____

Notes From This Week's Fellowship/Teaching: _____

_____
_____
_____
_____
_____
_____
_____
_____
_____
_____
_____
_____
_____
_____
_____
_____
_____
_____
_____
_____
_____
_____
_____
_____
_____
_____
_____

Personal Accountability Checklist: (if in a group, have someone else check you)

☐ I completed the character or command promise study.
☐ I read a chapter from the Book Of Proverbs each day.
☐ I journaled each day.

Lesson 20: Peace

A. Definition of peace: _____

_____

B. An example from my everyday life: _____

_____

C. A positive example from the Bible: Ps. 27:1-6; Luke 1:26-38; 2:25-32; John 14:25-31; Acts 27:21-25. _____

_____

D. A negative example from the Bible: 2 Sam. 15:1-13; Matt. 2:13-18; 26:69-75; 27:1-7; Luke 8:22-25. _____

E. Thinking about peace in my own life:

1. When have I demonstrated the quality of peace in a difficult time? _____

_____

2. In what situation did I fail to demonstrate peace? _____

_____

3. What problem in my life could God use to develop peace? _____

_____

4. Who can be a Christian model for me of peace? _____

_____

5. How can I develop this quality in my life? _____

_____

F. A scripture verse I will memorize to help build peace into my life: Isa. 26:3; Matt. 5:9; John 14:27; 16:33; Rom. 5:1; 12:18; Phil. 4:7. _____

_____

G. Self-evaluation:

1. Am I able to maintain peace even when circumstances are not peaceful?
2. When there are conflicts in relationships between my friends, do I help to restore peace?
3. Do I resist a critical, divisive spirit that destroys peace?
4. Am I willing to experience personal hurts in order to maintain peace?
5. Do I understand peace in the same way the Scriptures explain it?
6. Am I aware of those situations that usually rob me of peace?
7. Am I taking steps to deal with the root problem?
8. Do others consider me to be a peaceful individual?
9. Is this motto healthy: "Peace at any price"?
10. Is the kind of peace I am seeking really attainable?
11. Do I know how to attain that peace?
12. Does reading God's Word contribute to my inner peace?
13. Am I sometimes "uncomfortable" when everything seems peaceful?
14. Do I really want to be a peaceful person who brings peace to others?
15. Am I cooperating with God to make myself a person of peace?

Day 1: _____
_____
_____
_____
_____
_____
_____
_____
_____
_____
_____
_____
_____
_____

Day 2: _____
_____
_____
_____
_____
_____
_____
_____
_____
_____
_____
_____
_____

Day 3: _____
_____
_____
_____
_____
_____
_____
_____
_____
_____
_____
_____
_____
_____

Words Of Wisdom: read a chapter from the Book of Proverbs corresponding with today's date (if today is the seventh, read chapter seven from the Book of Proverbs.)

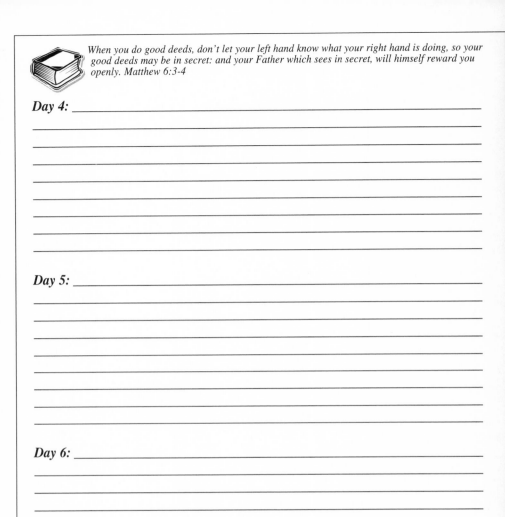

When you do good deeds, don't let your left hand know what your right hand is doing, so your good deeds may be in secret: and your Father which sees in secret, will himself reward you openly. Matthew 6:3-4

Day 4: _____

_____
_____
_____
_____
_____
_____
_____
_____
_____

Day 5: _____

_____
_____
_____
_____
_____
_____
_____
_____
_____

Day 6: _____

_____
_____
_____
_____
_____
_____
_____
_____
_____

Day 7: _____

_____
_____
_____
_____
_____
_____
_____
_____

Prayer Needs/Requests & How God Responded: _____

_____
_____
_____
_____
_____
_____
_____
_____
_____
_____
_____
_____
_____
_____
_____

Notes From This Week's Fellowship/Teaching: _____

_____
_____
_____
_____
_____
_____
_____
_____
_____
_____
_____
_____
_____
_____
_____
_____
_____
_____
_____
_____
_____
_____
_____
_____
_____
_____
_____

Personal Accountability Checklist: (if in a group, have someone else check you)
- ☐ I completed the character or command promise study.
- ☐ I read a chapter from the Book Of Proverbs each day.
- ☐ I journaled each day.

Lesson 21: Wisdom

A. Definition of wisdom: _____

_____

B. An example from my everyday life: _____

C. **A positive example from the Bible:** Gen. 37:39-45; 1 Kings 3:23-28; Dan. 2:17-24, 46-49; Matt. 22:15-45; Luke 2:41-52. _____

_____

D. **A negative example from the Bible:** Gen. 3:1-7; Ex. 32:1-3; 1 Sam. 25; Luke 12:15-21; Rom. 1:18-32. _____

E. **Thinking about wisdom in my own life:**

1. When have I been wise? _____

_____

2. In what situation did I fail to be wise? _____

_____

3. What problem in my life could God use to build wisdom? _____

_____

4. Who can be a Christian model for me of wisdom?_____

_____

5. How can I develop this quality in my life? _____

_____

F. **A scripture verse I will memorize to help build wisdom into my life:** Prov. 1:7; 4:5; 24:3; Col. 2:3; James 1:5, 6; 3:13. _____

_____

G. **Self-evaluation:**

1. Try to remember the last three decisions you made. Were they wise ones?
2. Do I seek advice from wise people to help me with major decisions?
3. Do I consider my parents to be wiser than I am?
4. Am I gaining in wisdom or in foolishness?
5. Do I envy people who seem to make wise choices consistently?
6. Does wisdom receive higher priority in my life than "happiness"?
7. Does reading and study increase wisdom?
8. Are people today generally wiser than people were 2,000 years ago?
9. Can I be successful without being wise?
10. Do I depend upon the Holy Spirit to guide me when making a decision?
11. Do I seek direction from the Scriptures when faced with alternatives?
12. Do I respect the advice of my parents, teachers, or pastor?
13. Am I convinced that the wisdom of the Bible is superior to the wisdom of this world?
14. Am I teachable? Do I readily listen to advice?
15. In conversation, am I interested in receiving wisdom from others or giving mine?
16. Am I convinced that all true wisdom comes from God?
17. Am I cooperating with God to make myself a wise person?

Day 1: _____
_____
_____
_____
_____
_____
_____
_____
_____
_____
_____
_____

Day 2: _____
_____
_____
_____
_____
_____
_____
_____
_____
_____
_____
_____
_____

Day 3: _____
_____
_____
_____
_____
_____
_____
_____
_____
_____
_____
_____
_____

 Words Of Wisdom: read a chapter from the Book of Proverbs corresponding with today's date (if today is the seventh, read chapter seven from the Book of Proverbs.)

Watch, and pray always, that you enter not into temptation and that you may be counted worthy to escape all these things that will come to pass, and to stand before the Son of man. Let not your heart be troubled, neither let it be afraid: you believe in God, believe also in me. Luke 21:36, John 14:1

Day 4: _____
_____
_____
_____
_____
_____
_____
_____
_____
_____

Day 5: _____
_____
_____
_____
_____
_____
_____
_____
_____
_____

Day 6: _____
_____
_____
_____
_____
_____
_____
_____
_____
_____

Day 7: _____
_____
_____
_____
_____
_____
_____
_____
_____
_____

Prayer Needs/Requests & How God Responded: _____
_____
_____
_____
_____
_____
_____
_____
_____
_____
_____
_____
_____
_____
_____

Notes From This Week's Fellowship/Teaching: _____
_____
_____
_____
_____
_____
_____
_____
_____
_____
_____
_____
_____
_____
_____
_____
_____
_____
_____
_____
_____
_____
_____
_____
_____
_____
_____

Personal Accountability Checklist: (if in a group, have someone else check you)
- ☐ I completed the character or command promise study.
- ☐ I read a chapter from the Book Of Proverbs each day.
- ☐ I journaled each day.

Lesson 22: Compassion

A. Definition of compassion: _____

_____

B. An example from my everyday life: _____

_____

C. A positive example from the Bible: 2 Sam. 9:1-13; Luke 10:25-37; 15:18-24; 18:35-43; 1 Cor. 13; 1 John 4:7-21. _____

_____

D. A negative example from the Bible: 1 Kings 12:12-15; 21:5-15; Matt. 18:23-35; John 19:1-16. _____

E. Thinking about compassion in my own life:

   1. When have I been compassionate? _____

   _____

   2. In what situation did I fail to be compassionate? _____

   _____

   3. What problem in my life could God use to build compassion? _____

   _____

   4. Who can be a Christian model for me of compassion? _____

   _____

   5. How can I develop this quality in my life? _____

   _____

F. A scripture verse I will memorize to help build compassion into my life: Prov. 10:12; Mark 12:29; John 15:12; Rom. 12:10; 1 Cor. 16:14; Col. 3:14; 1 John 4:18-21. _____

_____

G. Self-evaluation:

  1. When I feel compassionate, do I take positive action?

  2. Do I serve people out of compassion or out of duty?

  3. Does my pride sometimes prevent me from showing compassion?

  4. Do I ever consider a person weak if he or she shows compassion?

  5. Are girls generally more compassionate than boys?

  6. Do I feel guilty when I have refrained from showing compassion?

  7. Does the misery of others usually produce feelings of compassion in me?

  8. Do I sense conviction when I see people exhibiting much more compassion than I do?

  9. Am I willing to inconvenience myself to show compassion to someone in need?

  10. Am I able to show compassion to people whose problems irritate me?

  11. In what ways do I express compassion?

  12. Is loving others one of my chief goals in life?

  13. Am I cooperating with God to make myself an instrument of His perfect love?

Day 1: _____

_____
_____
_____
_____

_____
_____
_____
_____
_____
_____
_____
_____
_____

Day 2: _____

_____
_____
_____
_____
_____
_____
_____
_____
_____
_____
_____
_____
_____

Day 3: _____

_____
_____
_____
_____
_____
_____
_____
_____
_____
_____
_____
_____
_____

 Words Of Wisdom: read a chapter from the Book of Proverbs corresponding with today's date (if today is the seventh, read chapter seven from the Book of Proverbs.)

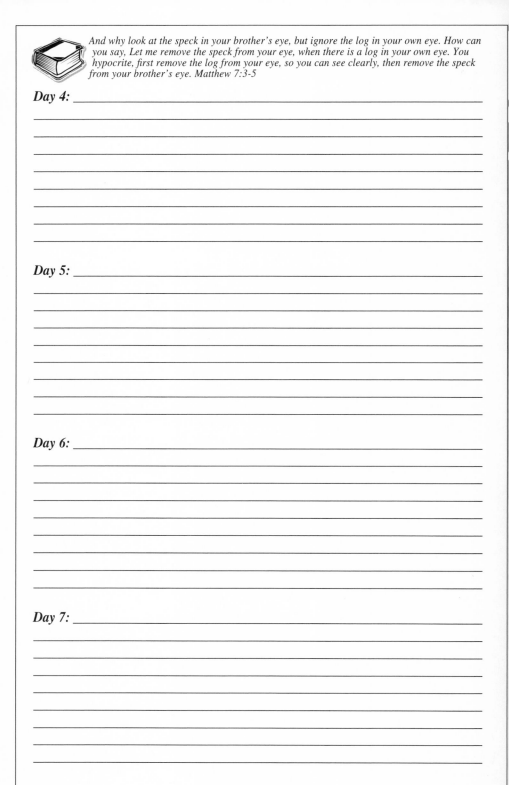

And why look at the speck in your brother's eye, but ignore the log in your own eye. How can you say, Let me remove the speck from your eye, when there is a log in your own eye. You hypocrite, first remove the log from your eye, so you can see clearly, then remove the speck from your brother's eye. Matthew 7:3-5

Day 4: _____

_____
_____
_____
_____
_____
_____
_____
_____

Day 5: _____

_____
_____
_____
_____
_____
_____
_____
_____

Day 6: _____

_____
_____
_____
_____
_____
_____
_____
_____

Day 7: _____

_____
_____
_____
_____
_____
_____
_____
_____

Prayer Needs/Requests & How God Responded: _____

_____

_____

_____

_____

_____

_____

_____

_____

_____

_____

_____

_____

_____

Notes From This Week's Fellowship/Teaching: _____

_____

_____

_____

_____

_____

_____

_____

_____

_____

_____

_____

_____

_____

_____

_____

_____

_____

_____

_____

_____

_____

_____

_____

Personal Accountability Checklist: (if in a group, have someone else check you)

☐ I completed the character or command promise study.

☐ I read a chapter from the Book Of Proverbs each day.

☐ I journaled each day.

Lesson 23: Fairness

A. Definition of fairness: _____

_____

B. An example from my everyday life: _____

_____

C. A positive example from the Bible: Lev. 19:13-18; Deut. 16:18-20; Acts 10:23-48; 15:6:11; Rom. 2:2-16. _____

_____

D. A negative example from the Bible: Isa. 53:1-12; Amos 5:11, 12; Luke 23:39-43; James 2:1-9. _____

E. Thinking about fairness in my own life:

   1. When have I been fair? _____

   _____

   2. In what situation did I fail to be fair? _____

   _____

   3. What problem in my life could God use to build fairness? _____

   _____

   4. Who can be a Christian model for me of fairness?_____

   _____

   5. How can I develop this quality in my life? _____

   _____

F. A scripture verse I will memorize to help build fairness into my life: Prov. 17:26; John 7:24; Acts 10:34; Rom 2:11; 10:12; James 2:1._____

_____

G. Self-evaluation:

   1. Do I expect others to be fair to me?

   2. How do I react when other people are treated unfairly?

   3. Do I experience greater fairness at home or with friends?

   4. Has God dealt fairly with your family?

   5. Is my life a testimony to the fairness of God?

   6. Do I believe that "all is fair in love and war"?

   7. Do different circumstances require varying degrees of fairness?

   8. Do I desire to be fair at all times?

   9. Do I consider God's answers to my prayers unfair?

  10. Am I treated fairly within my family, church, or school?

  11. Do I object to apparently unfair situations?

  12. How can fairness apply to international affairs?

Day 1: _____
_____
_____
_____
_____
_____
_____
_____
_____
_____
_____
_____
_____

Day 2: _____
_____
_____
_____
_____
_____
_____
_____
_____
_____
_____
_____
_____

Day 3: _____
_____
_____
_____
_____
_____
_____
_____
_____
_____
_____
_____
_____

 Words Of Wisdom: read a chapter from the Book of Proverbs corresponding with today's date (if today is the seventh, read chapter seven from the Book of Proverbs.)

You have heard it said, "An eye for an eye, and a tooth for a tooth": But I tell you not to resist evil: but whoever will hit you on the right cheek, turn to him the other also. And whoever compels you to go a mile, go two miles with him. Give to him that asks you, and don't turn your back on him that would borrow. Matthew 5:38-39, Matthew 5:41-42

Day 4: _____

_____

_____

_____

_____

_____

_____

_____

Day 5: _____

_____

_____

_____

_____

_____

_____

_____

_____

Day 6: _____

_____

_____

_____

_____

_____

_____

_____

_____

Day 7: _____

_____

_____

_____

_____

_____

_____

_____

_____

Prayer Needs/Requests & How God Responded: _____

_____
_____
_____
_____
_____
_____
_____
_____
_____
_____
_____
_____
_____
_____

Notes From This Week's Fellowship/Teaching: _____

_____
_____
_____
_____
_____
_____
_____
_____
_____
_____
_____
_____
_____
_____
_____
_____
_____
_____
_____
_____
_____
_____
_____
_____
_____
_____

Personal Accountability Checklist: (if in a group, have someone else check you)
- ☐ I completed the character or command promise study.
- ☐ I read a chapter from the Book Of Proverbs each day.
- ☐ I journaled each day.

Lesson 24: Enthusiasm

A. Definition of enthusiasm: _____

_____

B. An example from my everyday life: _____

_____

C. A positive example from the Bible: 2 Sam. 6:12-15; Neh. 2:17-20; John 2:13-17; Phil. 3:4-14. _____

_____

D. A negative example from the Bible: 1 Kings 19:4-10; Matt. 16:21-23; Luke 9:51-56; Rom. 10:1-4. _____

E. Thinking about enthusiasm in my own life:

1. When have I been enthusiastic? _____

_____

2. In what situation did I fail to be enthusiastic? _____

_____

3. What problem in my life could God use to build enthusiasm? _____

_____

4. Who can be a Christian model for me of enthusiasm? _____

_____

5. How can I develop this quality in my life? _____

_____

F. A scripture verse I will memorize to help build enthusiasm into my life: Matt. 5:16; Rom. 12:11; 1 Cor. 10:31; 15:58; Gal. 6:9; Col. 3:23. _____

_____

G. Self-evaluation:

1. Do my attitude and countenance show that I enjoy my work?
2. At home, do I have a positive spirit that makes me fun to be around, or am I a "sourpuss"?
3. Do I motivate others by getting excited about things they are involved in?
4. Do I greet others in a friendly manner when we meet?
5. Do I usually see disappointments as opportunities for God to "work all things for good"?
6. Can I distinguish true enthusiasm from emotional fervor?
7. Am I able to "rejoice with those who rejoice"? Am I genuinely happy when others succeed, even if they surpass my accomplishments?
8. Am I free in worship, or do I feel afraid to express my joy to God?
9. Does my enthusiasm result in positive involvement, or does it end with emotional expression?
10. Do enthusiastic people make me more enthusiastic or do they irritate me?
11. Am I secure in my enthusiasm? Can I be comfortable with my own enthusiasm?
12. Do I feel that people in general could use more enthusiasm in their lives?
13. Am I capable of generating more enthusiasm than I do now?
14. Am I willing to cooperate with God in becoming a more enthusiastic person?
15. On an "enthusiasm scale" of one to ten, where would I place myself?
16. Where would I like to be on the scale?

Day 1: _____
_____
_____
_____
_____
_____
_____
_____
_____
_____
_____
_____
_____

Day 2: _____
_____
_____
_____
_____
_____
_____
_____
_____
_____
_____
_____
_____

Day 3: _____
_____
_____
_____
_____
_____
_____
_____
_____
_____
_____
_____
_____
_____

 Words Of Wisdom: read a chapter from the Book of Proverbs corresponding with today's date (if today is the seventh, read chapter seven from the Book of Proverbs.)

Therefore if you bring your gift to the altar, and there remember, that your brother has something against you; leave your gift before the altar, and go first be reconciled to your brother, and then come and offer your gift. Matthew 5:23-24

Day 4: _____

_____
_____
_____
_____
_____
_____
_____
_____

Day 5: _____

_____
_____
_____
_____
_____
_____
_____
_____

Day 6: _____

_____
_____
_____
_____
_____
_____
_____
_____
_____

Day 7: _____

_____
_____
_____
_____
_____
_____
_____
_____
_____

Prayer Needs/Requests & How God Responded: _____

_____
_____
_____
_____
_____
_____
_____
_____
_____
_____
_____
_____
_____
_____

Notes From This Week's Fellowship/Teaching: _____

_____
_____
_____
_____
_____
_____
_____
_____
_____
_____
_____
_____
_____
_____
_____
_____
_____
_____
_____
_____
_____
_____
_____
_____
_____
_____
_____

Personal Accountability Checklist: (if in a group, have someone else check you)

☐ I completed the character or command promise study.
☐ I read a chapter from the Book Of Proverbs each day.
☐ I journaled each day.

Lesson 25: Initiative

A. Definition of initiative: _____

_____

B. An example from my everyday life: _____

_____

C. **A positive example from the Bible:** Gen. 1, 2; 1 Kings 9:10-28; Neh. 2; Matt. 14:22-33; Mark 2:1-5. _____

_____

D. **A negative example from the Bible:** Matt. 25:14-30; Luke 16:1-9; John 19:1-16; 2 Thess. 3:6-13. _____

E. **Thinking about initiative in my own life:**

1. When have I shown initiative? _____

_____

2. In what situation did I fail to show initiative? _____

_____

3. What problem in my life could God use to build initiative? _____

_____

4. Who can be a Christian model for me of initiative? _____

_____

5. How can I develop this quality in my life? _____

_____

F. **A scripture verse I will memorize to help build initiative into my life:** Gen. 1:1; Prov. 22:29; Eccles. 9:10; Phil. 3:14; 4:13. _____

_____

G. **Self-evaluation:**

1. Do I take responsibility for my own spiritual growth and not depend excessively upon others?
2. Do I make good use of my time?
3. Do I have hobbies that I enjoy?
4. When I see jobs that are not getting done, do I feel like doing them?
5. Do I attempt to make my friends successful in something?
6. Do I like to set goals and try to reach them?
7. When I have a "thousand things to do," am I able to choose one thing and do it, or do I get so discouraged I do nothing?
8. Am I convinced initiative is a mark of godliness?
9. Do I consider it my responsibility to encourage others?
10. Can I finish a job without having to be reminded or prodded?
11. Do I look for opportunities to witness about Jesus?
12. Am I especially creative in certain areas of my life?
13. Do I give special attention to new people who come to my church?
14. Do I carry out assignments or chores before being told?
15. Am I convinced God will develop initiative in me?

Day 1: _____
_____
_____
_____
_____
_____
_____
_____
_____
_____
_____
_____
_____

Day 2: _____
_____
_____
_____
_____
_____
_____
_____
_____
_____
_____
_____

Day 3: _____
_____
_____
_____
_____
_____
_____
_____
_____
_____
_____
_____
_____

 Words Of Wisdom: read a chapter from the Book of Proverbs corresponding with today's date (if today is the seventh, read chapter seven from the Book of Proverbs.)

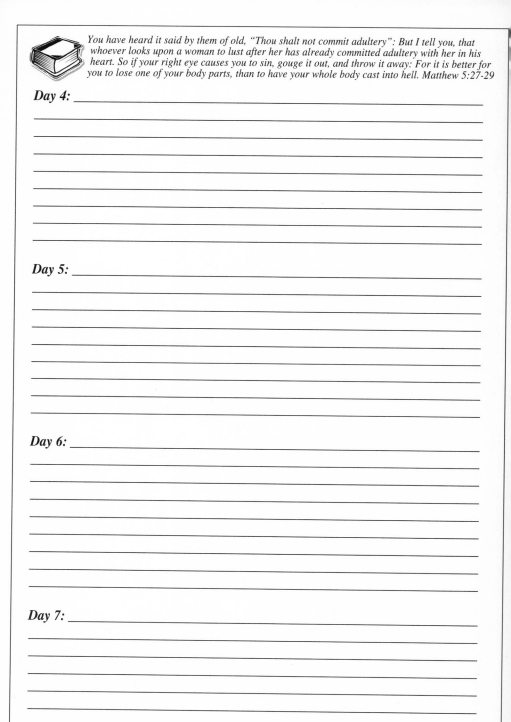

You have heard it said by them of old, "Thou shalt not commit adultery": But I tell you, that whoever looks upon a woman to lust after her has already committed adultery with her in his heart. So if your right eye causes you to sin, gouge it out, and throw it away: For it is better for you to lose one of your body parts, than to have your whole body cast into hell. Matthew 5:27-29

Day 4: _____

_____
_____
_____
_____
_____
_____
_____
_____
_____

Day 5: _____

_____
_____
_____
_____
_____
_____
_____
_____
_____

Day 6: _____

_____
_____
_____
_____
_____
_____
_____
_____
_____

Day 7: _____

_____
_____
_____
_____
_____
_____
_____
_____
_____

Prayer Needs/Requests & How God Responded: _____

_____

_____

_____

_____

_____

_____

_____

_____

_____

_____

_____

_____

_____

Notes From This Week's Fellowship/Teaching: _____

_____

_____

_____

_____

_____

_____

_____

_____

_____

_____

_____

_____

_____

_____

_____

_____

_____

_____

_____

_____

_____

_____

Personal Accountability Checklist: (if in a group, have someone else check you)
- ☐ I completed the character or command promise study.
- ☐ I read a chapter from the Book Of Proverbs each day.
- ☐ I journaled each day.

Lesson 26: Diligence

A. Definition of diligence: _____

_____

B. An example from my everyday life: _____

_____

C. A positive example from the Bible: Prov. 6:6-11; 31:10-31; Ruth 2:1-13; Mark 13:32-36; Acts 9:36-39. _____

_____

D. A negative example from the Bible: Prov. 24:30-34; 26:13-16; Matt. 25:1-13; Mark 14:32-42. _____

_____

E. Thinking about diligence in my own life:

1. When have I been diligent? _____

_____

2. In what situation did I fail to be diligent? _____

_____

3. What problem in my life could God use to make me more diligent? _____

_____

4. Who can be a Christian model for me of diligence? _____

_____

5. How can I develop this quality in my life? _____

_____

F. A scripture verse I will memorize to help build diligence into my life: Prov. 10:4; 13:4; Mark 13:33; Rom. 12:11; 1 Thess. 4:11; 2 Thess. 3:12; 2 Tim. 3:16. _____

_____

G. Self-evaluation:

1. Do I consider myself diligent?
2. Do my parents consider me diligent?
3. Is getting out of bed on time quite easy for me?
4. Am I diligent when the boss is not around?
5. Do I enjoy doing a job to the best of my ability?
6. Do people more diligent than I am make me feel guilty?
7. Do I see diligence as a positive quality or do I say when I see someone working hard, "Who is he trying to impress"?
8. Do I feel that diligent people are happier than lazy people?
9. Are the people I consider successful diligent?
10. Have I confessed laziness in my life?
11. Do I consider laziness a serious enough problem to be repented of, or does it rank low on my priorities?
12. Do I work with a sense of accountability to others, especially to God?
13. Do I have a daily devotional time?
14. Am I diligent in my work because I desire to honor God?
15. Do I carry out responsibilities in detail?
16. Do I want God to make me more diligent?

Day 1: _____
_____
_____
_____
_____
_____
_____
_____
_____
_____
_____
_____

Day 2: _____
_____
_____
_____
_____
_____
_____
_____
_____
_____
_____
_____
_____

Day 3: _____
_____
_____
_____
_____
_____
_____
_____
_____
_____
_____
_____
_____
_____

Words Of Wisdom: read a chapter from the Book of Proverbs corresponding with today's date (if today is the seventh, read chapter seven from the Book of Proverbs.)

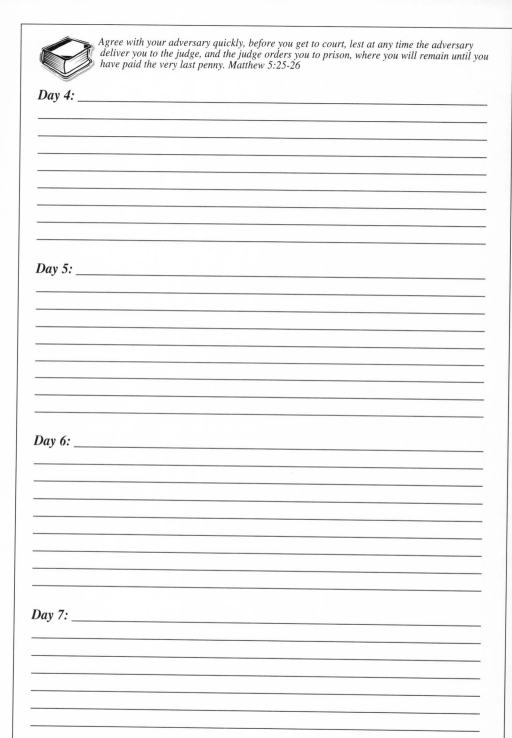

Agree with your adversary quickly, before you get to court, lest at any time the adversary deliver you to the judge, and the judge orders you to prison, where you will remain until you have paid the very last penny. Matthew 5:25-26

Day 4: _____

_____
_____
_____
_____
_____
_____
_____
_____

Day 5: _____

_____
_____
_____
_____
_____
_____
_____
_____
_____

Day 6: _____

_____
_____
_____
_____
_____
_____
_____
_____
_____

Day 7: _____

_____
_____
_____
_____
_____
_____
_____
_____

Prayer Needs/Requests & How God Responded: _____

_____

_____

_____

_____

_____

_____

_____

_____

_____

_____

_____

_____

_____

_____

Notes From This Week's Fellowship/Teaching: _____

_____

_____

_____

_____

_____

_____

_____

_____

_____

_____

_____

_____

_____

_____

_____

_____

_____

_____

_____

_____

_____

_____

_____

_____

_____

_____

_____

Personal Accountability Checklist: (if in a group, have someone else check you)

- ☐ I completed the character or command promise study.
- ☐ I read a chapter from the Book Of Proverbs each day.
- ☐ I journaled each day.

Lesson 27: Thoughtfulness

A. Definition of thoughtfulness: _____

_____

B. An example from my everyday life: _____

_____

C. **A positive example from the Bible:** Matt. 27:57-61; Mark 8:22-26; Luke 7:36-50; John 19:25-27; Phil. 1:19-30. _____

_____

D. **A negative example from the Bible:** Gen. 31:1-16; 1 Sam. 25:1-13; Jonah 4:1-11; Mark 10:13-16; Luke 15:25-32. _____

_____

E. **Thinking about thoughtfulness in my own life:**

1. When have I shown thoughtfulness? _____

_____

2. In what situation did I fail to be thoughtful? _____

_____

3. What problem in my life could God use to build thoughtfulness? _____

_____

4. Who can be a Christian model for me of thoughtfulness? _____

_____

5. How can I develop this quality in my life? _____

_____

F. **A scripture verse I will memorize to help build thoughtfulness into my life:** Matt. 10:42; Rom. 15:1, 2; Phil. 2:3, 4; Col. 3:14; 1 Pet. 3:7; 4:9; 1 John 3:18. _____

_____

G. **Self-evaluation:**

1. Do I remember the little details in people's lives that others tend to forget – birthdays, recent illnesses, prayer requests, favors?
2. Am I usually aware of when close friends are hurting?
3. Is meeting the needs of others more important to me than meeting my needs?
4. Do people seem to appreciate me because I am thoughtful?
5. Do I enjoy giving little "surprises" to others?
6. Do I often think about helping people in need?
7. Am I able to avoid critical thinking and complaining?
8. Do I resent being "stepped on" once in a while?
9. Have I ever confessed a lack of thoughtfulness?
10. Do I show appreciation to thoughtful people?
11. Is my thoughtfulness often inhibited by my laziness?
12. Is my thoughtfulness consistent?
13. Do I attempt to meet others' needs myself rather than expect someone else to?
14. Do I think of others even when I am in need?
15. Can I remember the last time I showed thoughtfulness?
16. Will I cooperate with God to make me a more thoughtful person?

Day 1: _____
_____
_____
_____
_____
_____
_____
_____
_____
_____
_____
_____
_____

Day 2: _____
_____
_____
_____
_____
_____
_____
_____
_____
_____
_____
_____
_____
_____

Day 3: _____
_____
_____
_____
_____
_____
_____
_____
_____
_____
_____
_____
_____
_____

 Words Of Wisdom: read a chapter from the Book of Proverbs corresponding with today's date (if today is the seventh, read chapter seven from the Book of Proverbs.)

If your brother trespass against you, rebuke him; and if he repent, forgive him. And if he trespass against you seven times in a day, and seven times in a day, turns to you and repents; you should forgive him. Luke 17:3-4

Day 4: _____

_____

_____

_____

_____

_____

_____

_____

_____

_____

Day 5: _____

_____

_____

_____

_____

_____

_____

_____

_____

_____

Day 6: _____

_____

_____

_____

_____

_____

_____

_____

_____

_____

Day 7: _____

_____

_____

_____

_____

_____

_____

_____

_____

_____

Prayer Needs/Requests & How God Responded: _____

_____
_____
_____
_____
_____
_____
_____
_____
_____
_____
_____
_____
_____

Notes From This Week's Fellowship/Teaching: _____

_____
_____
_____
_____
_____
_____
_____
_____
_____
_____
_____
_____
_____
_____
_____
_____
_____
_____
_____
_____
_____
_____
_____
_____
_____
_____
_____
_____

Personal Accountability Checklist: (if in a group, have someone else check you)

☐ I completed the character or command promise study.
☐ I read a chapter from the Book Of Proverbs each day.
☐ I journaled each day.

Lesson 28: Efficiency

A. Definition of efficiency: _____

_____

B. An example from my everyday life: _____

_____

C. A positive example from the Bible: Ex. 18:13-27; 35:30-36:7; Prov. 31:10-31; Luke 5:4-7; Acts 6:1-7; 1 Cor. 12:4-31; Eph. 4:11-16. _____

_____

D. A negative example from the Bible: Matt. 7:24-27; 25:14-30; Luke 13:6-9; 14:25-33; 15:11-17. _____

E. Thinking about efficiency in my own life:

1. When have I been efficient? _____

_____

2. In what situation did I fail to be efficient? _____

_____

3. What problem in my life could God use to build efficiency? _____

_____

4. Who can be a Christian model for me of efficiency? _____

_____

5. How can I develop this quality in my life? _____

_____

F. A scripture verse I will memorize to help build efficiency into my life: Ps. 90:12; Luke 7:21; Eph. 4:23; 5:15, 16; Col. 4:5; 1 Pet. 4:10. _____

_____

G. Self-evaluation:

1. Do I keep my room clean and orderly?
2. Am I on time for most of my appointments?
3. Am I often saying to myself, "I just don't have enough time"?
4. Do I enjoy keeping good records, lists of things to do, etc.?
5. Have I established my three highest priorities in life?
6. Does my daily schedule reflect my priorities?
7. Do I try to organize each day, or do I take each thing as it comes at me?
8. Do inefficient people frustrate me?
9. Is efficiency important to me?
10. Do I evaluate a task before I begin as well as after I finish?
11. Do I consider the cost of inefficiency?
12. Do I seek help to change an inefficient schedule?
13. Do I believe God is efficient?
14. Do I ever consider who pays for my inefficiency?
15. Are my close friends efficiency-conscious?
16. Would I like God to make me more efficient in my use of time?
17. Am I willing to cooperate with God to develop efficiency?

Day 1: _____

_____

_____

_____

_____

_____

_____

_____

_____

_____

_____

_____

Day 2: _____

_____

_____

_____

_____

_____

_____

_____

_____

_____

_____

_____

_____

Day 3: _____

_____

_____

_____

_____

_____

_____

_____

_____

_____

_____

_____

_____

Words Of Wisdom: read a chapter from the Book of Proverbs corresponding with today's date (if today is the seventh, read chapter seven from the Book of Proverbs.)

But when you fast, anoint your head, and wash your face, so it won't look like you are fasting to other people, only to your Father, which sees in secret, and He will reward you openly.
Matthew 6:17-18

Day 4: _____
_____
_____
_____
_____
_____
_____
_____
_____
_____
_____

Day 5: _____
_____
_____
_____
_____
_____
_____
_____
_____
_____
_____

Day 6: _____
_____
_____
_____
_____
_____
_____
_____
_____
_____
_____

Day 7: _____
_____
_____
_____
_____
_____
_____
_____
_____
_____

Prayer Needs/Requests & How God Responded: _____

_____
_____
_____
_____
_____
_____
_____
_____
_____
_____
_____
_____
_____

Notes From This Week's Fellowship/Teaching: _____

_____
_____
_____
_____
_____
_____
_____
_____
_____
_____
_____
_____
_____
_____
_____
_____
_____
_____
_____
_____
_____
_____
_____
_____

Personal Accountability Checklist: (if in a group, have someone else check you)
- ☐ I completed the character or command promise study.
- ☐ I read a chapter from the Book Of Proverbs each day.
- ☐ I journaled each day.

Lesson 29: Discretion

A. Definition of discretion: _____

_____

B. An example from my everyday life: _____

_____

C. **A positive example from the Bible:** Dan. 1:8-16; Matt. 21:23-27; Luke 2:15-19; Acts 15:6-30; Rom 14:13-23. _____

_____

D. **A negative example from the Bible:** Judges 11:29-40; Eccles. 5:1-7; Matt. 19:16-26; Luke 1:8-23; Gal. 2:1-5, 11-16. _____

_____

E. **Thinking about discretion in my own life:**

1. When have I shown discretion?_____

_____

2. In what situation did I fail to show discretion?_____

_____

3. What problem in my life could God use to build discretion? _____

_____

4. Who can be a Christian model for me of discretion? _____

_____

5. How can I develop this quality in my life? _____

_____

F. **A scripture verse I will memorize to help build discretion into my life:** Prov. 10:19; Eccles. 8:5; Rom. 12:2, 9; Rom 14:19 or 22; 1 Cor. 2:14 or 15; 8:9; Heb. 4:12; 5:14.

G. **Self-evaluation:**

1. When I choose my clothing, do I consider how people will respond?
2. Do I think it is important to avoid the appearance of evil as well as evil itself?
3. Are there activities which are not wrong in themselves but would be wrong for me?
4. When evaluating an activity, do I ask, "What's wrong with it?" Or "What is God's best for me?"
5. Do I want God's best, or do I just want to avoid doing what's wrong?
6. Do I feel pressured to do things because my friends are able to do them?
7. Do I think it is necessary to sometimes stand alone, even when I risk losing my friends?
8. When faced with difficult decisions, do I usually make the right one?
9. Do I listen carefully to the advice of those over me in the Lord?
10. Am I good at keeping secrets?
11. Do I have any secrets with the Lord?
12. Is my life an example of the saying, "Fools rush in where angels fear to tread"?
13. Do I have a standard for making judgments or decisions?
14. Is that standard a Biblical one?
15. Do I use the rule "When in doubt, don't"?
16. Will I cooperate with God to increase my discretion?

Day 1: _____
_____
_____
_____
_____
_____
_____
_____
_____
_____
_____
_____

Day 2: _____
_____
_____
_____
_____
_____
_____
_____
_____
_____
_____
_____

Day 3: _____
_____
_____
_____
_____
_____
_____
_____
_____
_____
_____
_____

 Words Of Wisdom: read a chapter from the Book of Proverbs corresponding with today's date (if today is the seventh, read chapter seven from the Book of Proverbs.)

Be merciful as your Father also is merciful, doing good, lending, hoping for nothing again; and your reward shall be great, and you will be the children of the Highest: for he is kind to the unthankful and to the evil. Luke 6:35-36

Day 4: _____
_____
_____
_____
_____
_____
_____
_____
_____

Day 5: _____
_____
_____
_____
_____
_____
_____
_____
_____

Day 6: _____
_____
_____
_____
_____
_____
_____
_____
_____

Day 7: _____
_____
_____
_____
_____
_____
_____
_____
_____

Prayer Needs/Requests & How God Responded: _____

_____

_____

_____

_____

_____

_____

_____

_____

_____

_____

_____

_____

_____

_____

_____

Notes From This Week's Fellowship/Teaching: _____

_____

_____

_____

_____

_____

_____

_____

_____

_____

_____

_____

_____

_____

_____

_____

_____

_____

_____

_____

_____

_____

_____

_____

_____

Personal Accountability Checklist: (if in a group, have someone else check you)
- ☐ I completed the character or command promise study.
- ☐ I read a chapter from the Book Of Proverbs each day.
- ☐ I journaled each day.

Lesson 30: Joy

A. Definition of joy: _____

_____

B. An example from my everyday life: _____

_____

C. A positive example from the Bible: Ex. 14:1-21; 1 Sam. 1:19, 2:10; Luke 10:17-21; 15:22-32; Acts 16:19-34. _____

_____

D. A negative example from the Bible: Ruth 1:19-21; Job 3:1-19; John 11:17-44. ___

_____

E. Thinking about joy in my own life:

1. When have I been especially joyful? _____

_____

2. In what situation did I fail to be joyful? _____

_____

3. What problem in my life could God use to build joy? _____

_____

4. Who can be a Christian model for me of joy? _____

_____

5. How can I develop this quality in my life? _____

_____

F. A scripture verse I will memorize to help build joy into my life: Ps. 16:11; 33:21; Luke 10:20; John 15:11; Rom. 14:17; Eph. 5:18, 19; Phil 4:4. _____

_____

G. Self-evaluation:

1. Some people are always grouchy when they get up. How do I act?
2. Am I joyful even when going through a difficult trial?
3. Do I avoid periods of depression or self-pity?
4. Does my joy depend on my relationship with God or on my circumstances?
5. Is my joy fragile – easily subject to change?
6. Does my family consider me a happy person?
7. When people are around me, do they "brighten up"?
8. Do I enjoy making other people happy?
9. Am I cheerful when I answer the phone, when I greet people on the street, or when I answer the door?
10. Does my joy reveal itself in my day-to-day contacts (schoolmates, mailman, neighbors)?
11. Do I make a point of being joyful when coming home or meeting friends?
12. Do I sing, whistle, dance or express joy in some way during my daily chores?
13. Do happy people annoy me?
14. Do I usually assume that "smiley" people are insincere?
15. Do I need more joy in my life?
16. Do I dare allow God to fill me with overflowing joy?

Day 1: _____
_____
_____
_____
_____
_____
_____
_____
_____
_____
_____
_____

Day 2: _____
_____
_____
_____
_____
_____
_____
_____
_____
_____
_____
_____

Day 3: _____
_____
_____
_____
_____
_____
_____
_____
_____
_____
_____
_____

Words Of Wisdom: read a chapter from the Book of Proverbs corresponding with today's date (if today is the seventh, read chapter seven from the Book of Proverbs.)

You have heard it said, Love your neighbor and hate your enemy. But I tell you, Love your enemies, bless them that curse you, do good to them that hate you, and pray for them which despitefully use you, and persecute you. Matthew 5:43-44

Day 4: _____

_____
_____
_____
_____
_____
_____
_____
_____

Day 5: _____

_____
_____
_____
_____
_____
_____
_____
_____
_____

Day 6: _____

_____
_____
_____
_____
_____
_____
_____
_____
_____

Day 7: _____

_____
_____
_____
_____
_____
_____
_____
_____

Prayer Needs/Requests & How God Responded: _____

_____
_____
_____
_____
_____
_____
_____
_____
_____
_____
_____
_____
_____

Notes From This Week's Fellowship/Teaching: _____

_____
_____
_____
_____
_____
_____
_____
_____
_____
_____
_____
_____
_____
_____
_____
_____
_____
_____
_____
_____
_____
_____
_____
_____
_____

Personal Accountability Checklist: (if in a group, have someone else check you)

- ☐ I completed the character or command promise study.
- ☐ I read a chapter from the Book Of Proverbs each day.
- ☐ I journaled each day.

Lesson 31: Optimism

A. Definition of optimism: _____

_____

B. An example from my everyday life: _____

_____

C. A positive example from the Bible: Num. 14:4-10; Hab. 3:17-19; Mark 14:53-62; Rom. 8:28-39; Phil. 3:12-15; Philemon 4:22._____

_____

D. A negative example from the Bible: Gen. 18:9-15; Num. 11:1-6; 13:25-33; John 5:2-9; 20:24-25. _____

_____

E. Thinking about optimism in my own life:

1. When have I been optimistic? _____

   _____

2. In what situation did I fail to be optimistic? _____

   _____

3. What problem in my life could God use to build optimism? _____

   _____

4. Who can be a Christian model for me of optimism? _____

   _____

5. How can I develop this quality in my life? _____

   _____

F. A scripture verse I will memorize to help build optimism into my life: Gen. 50:20; Luke 21:18; John 16:33; Rom. 8:25, 28; Phil. 4:8; 1 Thess. 5:18; Heb. 11:1. _____

_____

G. Self-evaluation:

1. Do I see good in every day regardless of the problems?
2. Do I usually think that life will be better in the future than it is now?
3. Have I seen positive results from the difficulties I have gone through?
4. Do I enjoy all kinds of weather?
5. Do I help others to see what God can do through their suffering?
6. Do pessimistic people irritate me?
7. Do I really expect God to sustain me in all my difficulties?
8. Am I confident in the abilities God has given me?
9. Does the future excite me?
10. Do I expect to have a good job, a good family, a successful marriage?
11. Do I criticize optimistic people?
12. Does my optimism increase when things are going well?
13. Am I convinced that optimism fits the Christian life-style better than pessimism?
14. Do I have a good reason to be optimistic about life?
15. Have I confessed negativism in my life? Do I want God to deal with it?
16. Am I cooperating with God to make myself optimistic?

Day 1: _____
_____
_____
_____
_____
_____
_____
_____
_____
_____
_____
_____
_____

Day 2: _____
_____
_____
_____
_____
_____
_____
_____
_____
_____
_____
_____
_____

Day 3: _____
_____
_____
_____
_____
_____
_____
_____
_____
_____
_____
_____
_____
_____

Words Of Wisdom: read a chapter from the Book of Proverbs corresponding with today's date (if today is the seventh, read chapter seven from the Book of Proverbs.)

If you continue in my Word, then you are my disciples indeed; and you will know the truth, and the truth will make you free. John 8:31-32

Day 4: _____

_____
_____
_____
_____
_____
_____
_____
_____

Day 5: _____

_____
_____
_____
_____
_____
_____
_____
_____

Day 6: _____

_____
_____
_____
_____
_____
_____
_____
_____

Day 7: _____

_____
_____
_____
_____
_____
_____
_____
_____

Prayer Needs/Requests & How God Responded: _____

_____

_____

_____

_____

_____

_____

_____

_____

_____

_____

_____

_____

_____

Notes From This Week's Fellowship/Teaching: _____

_____

_____

_____

_____

_____

_____

_____

_____

_____

_____

_____

_____

_____

_____

_____

_____

_____

_____

_____

_____

_____

Personal Accountability Checklist: (if in a group, have someone else check you)
- [ ] I completed the character or command promise study.
- [ ] I read a chapter from the Book Of Proverbs each day.
- [ ] I journaled each day.

Lesson 32: Obedience

A. Definition of obedience: _____

_____

B. An example from my everyday life: _____

_____

C. **A positive example from the Bible:** 2 Chron. 17:1-6; Acts 8:26-40; Phil. 2:1-11; James 1:22-25. _____

D. **A negative example from the Bible:** Josh. 7:16-21; 1 Sam. 15:17-23; Jonah 1:1-3; Matt. 15:1-9; Heb. 3:7-19. _____

E. **Thinking about obedience my own life:**

1. When have I been obedient? _____

_____

2. In what situation did I fail to be obedient? _____

_____

3. What problem in my life could God use to build obedience? _____

_____

4. Who can be a Christian model for me of obedience? _____

_____

5. How can I develop this quality in my life? _____

_____

F. **A scripture verse I will memorize to help build obedience into my life:** Prov. 19:16; Luke 11:28; John 14:15; 15:14; Eph. 2:10; 1 John 2:6; 2:17; 5:2. _____

_____

G. **Self-evaluation:**

1. Am I willing to do what God instructs regardless of the consequences?
2. Would my parents/leaders say that I am an obedient child/servant?
3. Do my teachers respect me because I have been obedient to them?
4. Do I experience joy in carrying out the desires of those over me?
5. Am I afraid of disobeying the will of God?
6. Do I grieve over my disobedience rather than just shrug it off?
7. Do I strive to be more obedient to the clear will of God in my life?
8. Do I feel hurt when a friend disobeys the Lord?
9. Do I have a clear conscience? Have I confessed disobedience and made any necessary restitution?
10. Do I feel that obedience is always the best way?
11. Do I expect others to obey me when I have a responsibility?
12. Is laziness one reason I disobey?
13. Do I argue to protect myself when I have disobeyed?
14. Have I been able to conquer areas of persistent disobedience?
15. If I were more obedient toward my parents/leaders, would it be easier for me to obey God in other areas?

Day 1: _____
_____
_____
_____
_____
_____
_____
_____
_____
_____
_____
_____
_____

Day 2: _____
_____
_____
_____
_____
_____
_____
_____
_____
_____
_____
_____
_____
_____
_____

Day 3: _____
_____
_____
_____
_____
_____
_____
_____
_____
_____
_____
_____
_____
_____
_____

Words Of Wisdom: read a chapter from the Book of Proverbs corresponding with today's date (if today is the seventh, read chapter seven from the Book of Proverbs.)

If any man comes to me, and hates not his father, and mother, and wife, and children, and brothers, and sisters, yes, and his own life also, cannot be my disciple. Luke 14:26

Day 4: _____
_____
_____
_____
_____
_____
_____
_____
_____
_____

Day 5: _____
_____
_____
_____
_____
_____
_____
_____
_____
_____

Day 6: _____
_____
_____
_____
_____
_____
_____
_____
_____
_____

Day 7: _____
_____
_____
_____
_____
_____
_____
_____
_____
_____

Prayer Needs/Requests & How God Responded: _____

_____
_____
_____
_____
_____
_____
_____
_____
_____
_____
_____
_____

Notes From This Week's Fellowship/Teaching: _____

_____
_____
_____
_____
_____
_____
_____
_____
_____
_____
_____
_____
_____
_____
_____
_____
_____
_____
_____
_____
_____
_____

Personal Accountability Checklist: (if in a group, have someone else check you)

- ☐ I completed the character or command promise study.
- ☐ I read a chapter from the Book Of Proverbs each day.
- ☐ I journaled each day.

Lesson 33: Reverence

A. Definition of reverence: _____
_____

B. An example from my everyday life: _____

C. **A positive example from the Bible:** Ex. 3:1-6; 1 Sam. 26:6-12; Ps. 34:1-14; Isa. 6:1-8; Rev. 4:6-11. _____
_____

D. **A negative example from the Bible:** 2 Sam. 16:20-23; Mal. 1:6-14; Matt. 21:33-43; Luke 23:39-43. _____

E. **Thinking about reverence in my own life:**

   1. When have I shown reverence? _____
   _____

   2. In what situation did I fail to be reverent? _____
   _____

   3. What problem in my life could God use to build reverence? _____
   _____

   4. Who can be a Christian model for me of reverence? _____
   _____

   5. How can I develop this quality in my life? _____
   _____

F. **A scripture verse I will memorize to help build reverence into my life:** Josh. 24:14; Ps. 25:12; 46:10; Prov. 1:7; 8:13; Eph. 6:5; Heb. 12:29. _____
_____

G. **Self-evaluation:**

   1. Do I respect traditions that are important to other people?
   2. Do I fear God when I have done wrong?
   3. Is worship a part of my daily schedule?
   4. Do I honor people much older than myself?
   5. Do I desire to be holy as God is holy?
   6. Do I regularly enjoy the presence of God with silence?
   7. Does my choice of slang expression demonstrate that I have a holy awe of God?
   8. Do I grieve when people take the Lord's name in vain?
   9. When I imagine God, do I see Him as great, majestic, awesome... a God to be feared?
   10. Am I selective with my reverence toward people?
   11. Do people need to earn my reverence?
   12. Do my close friends revere the things I revere?
   13. Are there ungodly things in my life that I revere?
   14. Do I desire to increase my reverence toward God and other people?
   15. Will I cooperate with God to increase this quality in my life?

Day 1: _____

_____

_____

_____

_____

_____

_____

_____

_____

_____

_____

Day 2: _____

_____

_____

_____

_____

_____

_____

_____

_____

_____

_____

_____

Day 3: _____

_____

_____

_____

_____

_____

_____

_____

_____

_____

_____

_____

Words Of Wisdom: read a chapter from the Book of Proverbs corresponding with today's date (if today is the seventh, read chapter seven from the Book of Proverbs.)

And when you pray, go in your closet, and when you shut the door, pray to your Father in secret, and your Father who sees in secret, will reward you openly. Matthew 6:6

Day 4: _____

_____
_____
_____
_____
_____
_____
_____
_____
_____

Day 5: _____

_____
_____
_____
_____
_____
_____
_____
_____
_____

Day 6: _____

_____
_____
_____
_____
_____
_____
_____
_____
_____

Day 7: _____

_____
_____
_____
_____
_____
_____
_____
_____
_____

Prayer Needs/Requests & How God Responded: _____

_____
_____
_____
_____
_____
_____
_____
_____
_____
_____
_____
_____
_____

Notes From This Week's Fellowship/Teaching: _____

_____
_____
_____
_____
_____
_____
_____
_____
_____
_____
_____
_____
_____
_____
_____
_____
_____
_____
_____
_____
_____
_____
_____
_____

Personal Accountability Checklist: (if in a group, have someone else check you)
- [ ] I completed the character or command promise study.
- [ ] I read a chapter from the Book Of Proverbs each day.
- [ ] I journaled each day.

Lesson 34: Faith

A. **Definition of faith:** _____

_____

B. **An example from my everyday life:** _____

_____

C. **A positive example from the Bible:** 2 Kings 5:8-14; Matt. 15:21-28; 21:18-22; Luke 7:1-10; Acts 3:1-10. _____

_____

D. **A negative example from the Bible:** Matt. 6:25-34; 14:22-33; 17:14-20; Mark 6:1-6; James 1:5-8. _____

E. **Thinking about faith my own life:**

1. When have I shown faith? _____

_____

2. In what situation did I fail to show faith? _____

_____

3. What problem in my life could God use to build faith? _____

_____

4. Who can be a Christian model for me of faith? _____

_____

5. How can I develop this quality in my life? _____

_____

F. **A scripture verse I will memorize to help build faith into my life:** Ps. 40:4; 118:8; Matt. 21:22; 1 Cor. 2:5; Eph. 2:8; Heb. 11:1; James 1:6. _____

_____

G. **Self-evaluation:**

1. Have I seen many of my prayers answered?
2. Do I pray because I believe God likes to answer prayers?
3. When prayers are not answered, am I usually discouraged?
4. Do I get excited about trusting God for all my needs?
5. Am I confident that God will meet all my financial needs?
6. Have I given sacrificially and seen God restore everything I'd given?
7. Does my life and testimony encourage faith in others?
8. Do trials increase my faith?
9. Do I have more faith in my ability than in God's?
10. Do testimonies of other people increase my faith?
11. Is my faith weakened when others try to discourage me?
12. Do I have faith to obey when God shows me a need that I should meet?
13. Are my friends examples of faith-filled living?

Day 1: _____
_____
_____
_____
_____

_____
_____
_____
_____
_____
_____
_____

Day 2: _____
_____
_____
_____
_____
_____
_____
_____
_____
_____
_____
_____

Day 3: _____
_____
_____
_____
_____
_____
_____
_____
_____
_____
_____
_____
_____

Words Of Wisdom: read a chapter from the Book of Proverbs corresponding with today's date (if today is the seventh, read chapter seven from the Book of Proverbs.)

This is my commandment, that you love one another, as I have loved you. John 15:12

Day 4: _____

_____
_____
_____
_____
_____
_____
_____
_____
_____

Day 5: _____

_____
_____
_____
_____
_____
_____
_____
_____
_____

Day 6: _____

_____
_____
_____
_____
_____
_____
_____
_____
_____

Day 7: _____

_____
_____
_____
_____
_____
_____
_____
_____
_____

Prayer Needs/Requests & How God Responded: _____

_____
_____
_____
_____
_____
_____
_____
_____
_____
_____
_____
_____
_____
_____
_____
_____

Notes From This Week's Fellowship/Teaching: _____

_____
_____
_____
_____
_____
_____
_____
_____
_____
_____
_____
_____
_____
_____
_____
_____
_____
_____
_____
_____
_____
_____
_____
_____
_____
_____

Personal Accountability Checklist: (if in a group, have someone else check you)

- ☐ I completed the character or command promise study.
- ☐ I read a chapter from the Book Of Proverbs each day.
- ☐ I journaled each day.

Lesson 35: The Commandment To Live A Repentant Life

1. **Repent Or Jesus Will Remove The Lamp Stand (spiritual light):** "From that time on Jesus began to preach, 'Repent, for the kingdom of heaven is near.' " Matthew 4:17 "Remember the height from which you have fallen! Repent and do the things you did at first. If you do not repent, I will come to you and remove your lamp stand from its place." Revelation 2:5

2. **First Find And Do Kingdom Ways, Then Receive:** "But seek first his kingdom and his righteousness, and all these things will be given to you as well." Matthew 6:33

3. **Ask, Seek, Knock:** "Ask and it will be given to you; seek and you will find; knock and the door will be opened to you." Matthew 7:7

4. **Come To Christ To Receive Rest:** "Come to me, all you who are weary and burdened, and I will give you rest." Matthew 11:28

5. **Following Jesus Requires Self Denial and Personal Crucifixion:** "Then Jesus said to his disciples, 'If anyone would come after me, he must deny himself and take up his cross and follow me.' " Matthew 16:24

6. **Give Forgiveness To Receive More:** "And when you stand praying, if you hold anything against anyone, forgive him, so that your Father in heaven may forgive you your sins." Mark 11:25

7. **Obedience To His Commands Opens The Narrow Door To Heaven:** "Make every effort to enter through the narrow door, because many, I tell you, will try to enter and will not be able to." Luke 13:24

The Promise Of Eternal Life For Believers

1. **Whoever Comes To Christ Will Not Be Driven Away:** "I am the bread of life, He who comes to me will never go hungry, and he who believes in me will never be thirsty. But as I told you, you have seen me and still you do not believe. All the Father gives me will come to me, and whoever comes to me I will never drive away." John 6:35-37

2. **Shall Not Perish:** "Just as Moses lifted up the snake in the desert, so the Son of Man must be lifted up, that everyone who believes in him may have eternal life. For God so loved the world that he gave his one and only Son, that whoever believes in him shall not perish but have eternal life." John 3:14-16

3. **Has Crossed Over From Death To Life:** "I tell you the truth, whoever hears my word and believes him who sent me has eternal life and will not be condemned; he has crossed over from death to life." John 5:24

4. **Will Be Raised At The Last Day:** "For my Father's will is that everyone who looks to the Son and believes in him shall have eternal life, and I will raise him up at the last day." John 6:40

5. **Has Everlasting Life:** "I tell you the truth, he who believes has everlasting life." John 6:47

6. **Will Never Die:** "Jesus said to her, I am the resurrection and the life. He who believes in me will live, even though he dies; and whoever lives and believes in me will never die. Do you believe this?" John 6:25-26

7. **Will Be Saved:** "Whoever believes and is baptized will be saved, but whoever does not believe will be condemned." Mark 16:16

Day 1: _____

_____

_____

_____

_____

_____

_____

_____

_____

_____

_____

Day 2: _____

_____

_____

_____

_____

_____

_____

_____

_____

_____

_____

Day 3: _____

_____

_____

_____

_____

_____

_____

_____

_____

_____

_____

_____

Words Of Wisdom: read a chapter from the Book of Proverbs corresponding with today's date (if today is the seventh, read chapter seven from the Book of Proverbs.)

My food and nourishment is to do the will of him that sent me, and to finish his work. I can of my own self do nothing: as I hear, I judge: and my judgement is just; because I seek not my will, but the will of the Father which sent me. John 4:34; John 5:30.

Day 4: _____

_____
_____
_____
_____
_____
_____
_____
_____

Day 5: _____

_____
_____
_____
_____
_____
_____
_____
_____

Day 6: _____

_____
_____
_____
_____
_____
_____
_____
_____

Day 7: _____

_____
_____
_____
_____
_____
_____
_____

Prayer Needs/Requests & How God Responded: _____

_____

_____

_____

_____

_____

_____

_____

_____

_____

_____

_____

_____

_____

Notes From This Week's Fellowship/Teaching: _____

_____

_____

_____

_____

_____

_____

_____

_____

_____

_____

_____

_____

_____

_____

_____

_____

_____

_____

_____

_____

_____

_____

_____

_____

Personal Accountability Checklist: (if in a group, have someone else check you)

☐ I completed the character or command promise study.
☐ I read a chapter from the Book Of Proverbs each day.
☐ I journaled each day.

Lesson 36: The Commandment To Be Christ's Witness In Holy Spirit Power

1. **Receive The Holy Spirit:** "And with that he breathed on them and said, 'Receive the Holy Spirit.' " John 20:22

2. **Let God's Children First Be Filled:** " 'First let the children eat all they want,' he told her, 'For it is not right to take the children's bread and toss it to their dogs.' " Mark 7:27

3. **To Drink, You Must Be Thirsty:** "On the last and greatest day of the Feast, Jesus stood and said in a loud voice, 'If anyone is thirsty, let him come to me and drink. Whoever believes in me, as the Scripture has said, streams of living water will flow from within him.' " John 7:37-38

4. **Obeying His Commandments Prepares The Way To Receive The Counselor:** "If you love me, you will obey what I command. And I will ask the Father, and he will give you another Counselor to be with you forever – the Spirit of truth. The world cannot accept him, because it neither sees him nor knows him. But you know him, for he lives with you and will be in you." John 14:15-17

5. **Ask In His Name And Receive Full Joy:** "Until now you have not asked for anything in my name. Ask and you will receive, and your joy will be complete." John 16:24

6. **We Must Be Spirit Filled To Witness:** "I am going to send you what my Father has promised; but stay in the city until you have been clothed with power from on high." Luke 24:49

7. **We Must Testify Of Christ:** "When the Counselor comes, whom I will send to you from the Father, The Spirit of truth who goes out from the Father, he will testify about me. And you also must testify, for you have been with me from the beginning." John 15:26-27

Promises Of The Father's Gift Of The Holy Spirit

1. **A Gift To Those That Ask:** "If you then, though you are evil, know how to give good gifts to your children, how much more will your Father in heaven give the Holy Spirit to those who ask him!" Luke 11:13

2. **The Well Of Life:** "...but whoever drinks the water I give him will never thirst. Indeed, the water I give him will become in him a spring of water welling up to eternal life." John 4:14

3. **Living Water Flowing From Within:** "...as the Scripture has said, streams of living water will flow from within him. By this he meant the Spirit..." John 7:37-39

4. **The True Spirit Counselor With Us Forever:** "...he will give you another Counselor to be with you forever – the Spirit of truth..." John 14:16-17

5. **The Offer Of Breath And The Holy Spirit:** "And with that he breathed on them and said, 'Receive the Holy Spirit.' " John 20:22

6. **The Promised Clothing Of Power:** "I am going to send you what my Father has promised; but stay in the city until you have been clothed with power from on high." Luke 24:49

7. **The Baptism With The Holy Spirit:** "For John baptized with water, but in a few days you will be baptized with the Holy Spirit." Acts 1:5

Day 1: _____
_____
_____
_____
_____
_____
_____
_____
_____
_____
_____
_____

Day 2: _____
_____
_____
_____
_____
_____
_____
_____
_____
_____
_____
_____

Day 3: _____
_____
_____
_____
_____
_____
_____
_____
_____
_____
_____
_____

Words Of Wisdom: read a chapter from the Book of Proverbs corresponding with today's date (if today is the seventh, read chapter seven from the Book of Proverbs.)

If any man will come after me, let him deny himself, and take up his cross daily, and follow me. Luke 9:23

Day 4: _____

_____
_____
_____
_____
_____
_____
_____
_____

Day 5: _____

_____
_____
_____
_____
_____
_____
_____
_____

Day 6: _____

_____
_____
_____
_____
_____
_____
_____
_____

Day 7: _____

_____
_____
_____
_____
_____
_____
_____
_____

Prayer Needs/Requests & How God Responded: _____

_____

_____

_____

_____

_____

_____

_____

_____

_____

_____

_____

_____

_____

Notes From This Week's Fellowship/Teaching: _____

_____

_____

_____

_____

_____

_____

_____

_____

_____

_____

_____

_____

_____

_____

_____

_____

_____

_____

_____

_____

_____

_____

Personal Accountability Checklist: (if in a group, have someone else check you)
☐ I completed the character or command promise study.
☐ I read a chapter from the Book Of Proverbs each day.
☐ I journaled each day.

Lesson 37: The Commandment To Share The Gospel

1. **Share The Gospel (good news):** "As you go, preach this message: The Kingdom of heaven is near." Matthew 10:7. "He said to them, 'Go into all the world and preach the good news to all creation.' " Mark 16:15

2. **Freely Give:** "Heal the sick, raise the dead, cleanse those who have leprosy, drive out demons. Freely you have received, freely give." Matthew 10:8

3. **Call All Into Discipleship:** "Therefore go and make disciples of all nations, baptizing them in the name of the Father and of the Son and of the Holy Spirit," Matthew 28:19

4. **Teach Them To Obey:** "...and teaching them to obey everything I have commanded you. And surely I am with you always, to the very end of the age." Matthew 28:20

5. **Bring Into The Open Whatever Is Concealed:** "For whatever is hidden is meant to be disclosed, and whatever is concealed is meant to be brought out into the open." Mark 4:22

6. **Begin Where You Are:** "He told them, 'This is what is written: The Christ will suffer and rise from the dead on the third day, and repentance and forgiveness of sins will be preached in his name to all nations, beginning at Jerusalem.' " Luke 24:46-47

7. **Three Categories Of Sharing:** "When they had finished eating, Jesus said to Simon Peter, 'Simon, son of John, do you truly love me more than these?' 'Yes Lord,' he said, 'You know that I love you.' Jesus said, 'Feed my lambs.' Again Jesus said, 'Simon, son of John, do you truly love me?' He answered, 'Yes Lord, you know that I love you.' Jesus said, 'Take care of my sheep.' The third time he said to him, 'Simon, son of John, do you love me?' Peter was hurt because Jesus asked him the third time, 'Do you love me?' He said, 'Lord, you know all things; you know that I love you.' Jesus said, 'Feed my sheep.' " John 21:15-17

Promises Of The Holy Spirit's Activity

1. **He Convicts Of Sin, Righteousness, Judgement and Guilt:** "When he comes, he will convict the world of guilt in regard to sin and righteousness and judgment." John 16:8

2. **He Spiritually Births Like The Wind Blows:** "The wind blows where ever it pleases. You hear its sound, but you cannot tell where it comes from or where it is going. So it is with everyone born of the Spirit." John 3:8

3. **He Gives Life:** "The Spirit gives life; the flesh counts for nothing. The words I have spoken to you are spirit and they are life." John 6:63

4. **He Testifies About Christ:** "When the Counselor comes, whom I will send to you from the Father, the Spirit of truth who goes out from the Father, he will testify about me." John 15:26

5. **He Teaches And Reminds Of Christ's Words:** "But the Counselor, the Holy Spirit, whom the Father will send in my name, will teach you all things and will remind you of everything I have said to you." John 14:26

6. **He Gives Guidance And Advance Notice:** "But when he, the Spirit of Truth comes, he will guide you into all truth. He will not speak on his own; he will speak only what he hears, and he will tell you what is yet to come." John 16:13

7. **To The Receiver, He Gives Power To Witness:** "But you will receive power when the Holy Spirit comes on you; and you will be my witnesses in Jerusalem, and in all Judea and Samaria, and to the ends of the earth." Acts 1:8

Day 1: _____
_____
_____
_____
_____
_____
_____
_____
_____
_____
_____
_____

Day 2: _____
_____
_____
_____
_____
_____
_____
_____
_____
_____
_____
_____
_____

Day 3: _____
_____
_____
_____
_____
_____
_____
_____
_____
_____
_____
_____
_____

 Words Of Wisdom: read a chapter from the Book of Proverbs corresponding with today's date (if today is the seventh, read chapter seven from the Book of Proverbs.)

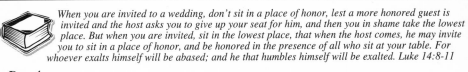

When you are invited to a wedding, don't sit in a place of honor, lest a more honored guest is invited and the host asks you to give up your seat for him, and then you in shame take the lowest place. But when you are invited, sit in the lowest place, that when the host comes, he may invite you to sit in a place of honor, and be honored in the presence of all who sit at your table. For whoever exalts himself will be abased; and he that humbles himself will be exalted. Luke 14:8-11

Day 4: _____
_____
_____
_____
_____
_____
_____
_____
_____

Day 5: _____
_____
_____
_____
_____
_____
_____
_____
_____

Day 6: _____
_____
_____
_____
_____
_____
_____
_____
_____

Day 7: _____
_____
_____
_____
_____
_____
_____
_____
_____

Prayer Needs/Requests & How God Responded: _____

_____
_____
_____
_____
_____
_____
_____
_____
_____
_____
_____
_____
_____
_____

Notes From This Week's Fellowship/Teaching: _____

_____
_____
_____
_____
_____
_____
_____
_____
_____
_____
_____
_____
_____
_____
_____
_____
_____
_____
_____
_____
_____
_____
_____
_____

Personal Accountability Checklist: (if in a group, have someone else check you)
- ☐ I completed the character or command promise study.
- ☐ I read a chapter from the Book Of Proverbs each day.
- ☐ I journaled each day.

Lesson 38: The Commandment To Grow Into Mature Love

1. Suffer Now To Win Later: "But I tell you, do not resist an evil person. If someone strikes you on the right cheek, turn to him the other also. And If someone wants to sue you and take your tunic, let him have your cloak as well. If someone forces you to go one mile, go with him two miles." Matthew 5:39-41

2. **His Love In Us Is Our Weapon:** "But I tell you, 'Love your enemies and pray for those who persecute you…' " Matthew 5:44 'Put your sword back in its place,' Jesus said to him, 'for all who draw the sword will die by the sword.' " Matthew 26:52

3. **Become Like Our Father:** "Be perfect, therefore, as your heavenly Father is perfect." Matthew 5:48

4. **How To Become Mature:** "Jesus answered, 'If you want to be perfect, go, sell your possessions and give to the poor, and you will have treasure in heaven. Then come, follow me.' " Matthew 19:21 "Do not be afraid, little flock, for your Father has been pleased to give you the kingdom. Sell your possessions and give to the poor. Provide purses for yourselves that will not wear out, a treasure in heaven that will not be exhausted, where no thief comes near and no moth destroys." Luke 12:32-33

5. **Love, Do Good, Bless And Pray:** "But I tell you who hear me, 'Love your enemies, do good to those who hate you, bless those who curse you, pray for those who mistreat you.' " Luke 6:27-28

6. **Lend Without Expectation:** "But love your enemies, do good to them, and lend to them without expecting to get anything back. Then your reward will be great, and you will be sons of the Most High, because he is kind to the ungrateful and wicked." Luke 6:35

7. **Stand Firm Now To Gain Later:** "By standing firm you will gain life." Luke 21:19

Promises Of Power To Overcome Satan's Activities

1. **All Harm Is Prevented By Exercising Christ's Authority:** "…I have given you authority to trample on snakes and scorpions and to overcome all the power of the enemy; nothing will harm you." Luke 10:18-19

2. **Binding And Loosening:** "…whatever you bind on earth…loose on earth…" Matthew 18:18

3. **At Times, Believers Drive Out Demons In Christ's Name:** "And these signs will accompany those who believe: In my name they will drive out demons." Mark 16:17

4. **At Times, Believers Fast And Pray To Minister:** "But this kind does not go out except by prayer and fasting." Matthew 17:21

5. **Satan Has Been Judged And Defeated At Calvary:** "Now is the time for judgment on this world; now the prince of this world will be driven out." John 12:31

6. **Christ Frees Completely:** "So if the Son sets you free, you will be free indeed." John 8:36

7. **Illnesses Placed By Satan Should Be Removed By God's Power:** "Then should not this woman, a daughter of Abraham, whom Satan has kept bound for eighteen long years, be set free on the Sabbath day from what bound her?" Luke 13:16

Day 1: _____
_____
_____
_____
_____
_____
_____
_____
_____
_____
_____
_____

Day 2: _____
_____
_____
_____
_____
_____
_____
_____
_____
_____
_____
_____
_____
_____

Day 3: _____
_____
_____
_____
_____
_____
_____
_____
_____
_____
_____
_____
_____
_____

Words Of Wisdom: read a chapter from the Book of Proverbs corresponding with today's date (if today is the seventh, read chapter seven from the Book of Proverbs.)

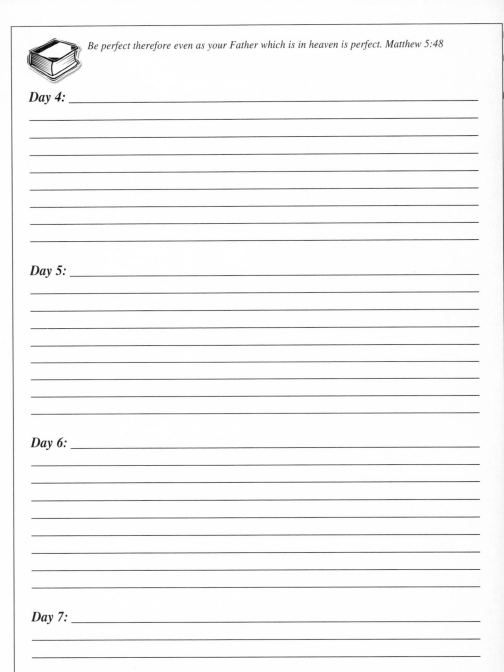

Be perfect therefore even as your Father which is in heaven is perfect. Matthew 5:48

Day 4: _____

_____
_____
_____
_____
_____
_____
_____
_____
_____

Day 5: _____

_____
_____
_____
_____
_____
_____
_____
_____
_____

Day 6: _____

_____
_____
_____
_____
_____
_____
_____
_____
_____

Day 7: _____

_____
_____
_____
_____
_____
_____
_____
_____
_____

Prayer Needs/Requests & How God Responded: _____

_____
_____
_____
_____
_____
_____
_____
_____
_____
_____
_____
_____
_____
_____

Notes From This Week's Fellowship/Teaching: _____

_____
_____
_____
_____
_____
_____
_____
_____
_____
_____
_____
_____
_____
_____
_____
_____
_____
_____
_____
_____
_____
_____
_____
_____

Personal Accountability Checklist: (if in a group, have someone else check you)
- ☐ I completed the character or command promise study.
- ☐ I read a chapter from the Book Of Proverbs each day.
- ☐ I journaled each day.

Lesson 39: The Commandment To Be Salt And Light

1. **Do Good Deeds Daily:** "In the same way, let your light shine before men, that they may see your good deeds and praise your Father in heaven." Matthew 5:16

2. **Minister First To Your Own Family:** "Jesus did not let him, but said, 'Go home to your family and tell them how much the Lord has done for you, and how he has had mercy on you.' " Mark 5:19

3. **Give God's Mercy To Others:** "Be merciful, just as your Father is merciful." Luke 6:36

4. **Check Your Own Guidance:** "See to it, then, that the light within you is not darkness." Luke 11:35

5. **See The Lost Souls Around You Today:** "Do you not say, 'Four months more and then the harvest?' I tell you, open your eyes and look at the fields! They are ripe for harvest." John 4:35

6. **Serve Him Now:** "Then Jesus told them, 'You are going to have the light just a little while longer. Walk while you have the light, before darkness overtakes you. The man who walks in the dark does not know where he is going.' " John 12:35

7. **Fruit Bearers Get Prayer Results:** "This is to my Father's glory, that you bear much fruit, showing yourselves to be my disciples." John 15:8 "You did not choose me, but I chose you and appointed you to go and bear fruit – fruit that will last. Then the Father will give you whatever you ask in my name." John 15:16

Promises Of God's Supernatural Protection

1. **Jesus Calls His Own To Close Relationship:** "I am the good shepherd; I know my sheep and my sheep know me." John 10:14

2. **No One Can Snatch Us From Jesus' Hand:** "I give them eternal life, and they shall never perish, no one can snatch them out of my hand." John 10:28

3. **No One Can Snatch Us From Our Father's Hand:** "My Father, who has given them to me, is greater than all; no one can snatch them out of my Father's hand." John 10:29

4. **Jesus Keeps His Own And Raises Them From Death:** "And this is the will of Him who sent me, that I shall lose none of all that He has given me, but raise them up at the last day." John 6:39

5. **Through His Name Jesus Protects:** "While I was with them, I protected them and kept them safe by that name you gave me…" John 17:12a

6. **End Time Protection Is Provided:** "If the Lord had not cut short those days, no one would survive." Mark 13:20

7. **Angelic Protection:** "See that you do not look down on one of these little ones. For I tell you that their angels in heaven always see the face of my Father in heaven." Matthew 18:10

Day 1: _____
_____
_____
_____
_____
_____
_____
_____
_____
_____
_____
_____

Day 2: _____
_____
_____
_____
_____
_____
_____
_____
_____
_____
_____
_____

Day 3: _____
_____
_____
_____
_____
_____
_____
_____
_____
_____
_____
_____
_____

 Words Of Wisdom: read a chapter from the Book of Proverbs corresponding with today's date (if today is the seventh, read chapter seven from the Book of Proverbs.)

If you abide in me, and my words abide in you, you shall ask what you will, and it will be done for you. John 15:7

Day 4: _____

_____
_____
_____
_____
_____
_____
_____
_____

Day 5: _____

_____
_____
_____
_____
_____
_____
_____
_____

Day 6: _____

_____
_____
_____
_____
_____
_____
_____
_____

Day 7: _____

_____
_____
_____
_____
_____
_____
_____
_____

Prayer Needs/Requests & How God Responded: _____

_____

_____

_____

_____

_____

_____

_____

_____

_____

_____

_____

_____

_____

Notes From This Week's Fellowship/Teaching: _____

_____

_____

_____

_____

_____

_____

_____

_____

_____

_____

_____

_____

_____

_____

_____

_____

_____

_____

_____

_____

_____

_____

_____

_____

_____

Personal Accountability Checklist: (if in a group, have someone else check you)

- ☐ I completed the character or command promise study.
- ☐ I read a chapter from the Book Of Proverbs each day.
- ☐ I journaled each day.

Lesson 40: The Commandment To Totally Love God

1. **Don't Foolishly Test God:** "Jesus answered him, 'It is written, Do not put the Lord your God to the test.' " Matthew 4:7

2. **Worship And Serve Only The Lord God:** "Jesus said to him, 'Away from me, Satan!' For it is written: 'Worship the Lord Your God, and serve him only.' " Matthew 4:10

3. **Call No Man On Earth Father:** "And do not call anyone on earth 'father', for you have one Father, and he is in heaven." Matthew 23:9

4. **Love The Lord God Totally:** "Love the Lord your God with all your heart and with all your soul and with all your mind and with all your strength." Mark 12:30

5. **Fear Almighty God:** "But I will show you whom you should fear. Fear him who, after the killing of the body, has power to throw you into hell. Yes, I tell you, fear him." Luke 12:5

6. **Worship The Father In Spirit And In Truth:** "Yet a time is coming and has now come when the true worshipers will worship the Father in spirit and truth, for they are the kind of worshipers the Father seeks." John 4:23

7. **Honor Jesus And You Honor Our Father:** "Moreover, the Father judges no one, but has entrusted all judgment to the Son, that all may honor the Son just as they honor the Father. He who does not honor the Son does not honor the Father, who sent him." John 5:22-23

Promises To One Mistreated For Living And Speaking Like Christ

1. **Great Heavenly Rewards:** "Blessed are those who are persecuted because of righteousness, for theirs is the kingdom of heaven. Blessed are you when people insult you, persecute you and falsely say all kinds of evil against you because of me. Rejoice and be glad, because great is your reward in heaven, for in the same way they persecuted the prophets who were before you." Matthew 5: 10-12

2. **The Faithful Will Be Saved:** "All men will hate you because of me, but he who stands firm to the end will be saved." Matthew 10:22

3. **Not A Hair On The Head Of The Faithful Will Perish:** "You will be betrayed even by parents, brothers, relatives and friends, and they will put some of you to death. All men will hate you because of me. But not a hair of your head will perish. By standing firm you will gain life." Luke 21:16-19

4. **Words And Wisdom Received When Needed:** "But before all this, they will lay hands on you and persecute you. They will deliver you to synagogues and prisons, and you will be brought before kings and governors, and all on account of my name. This will result in your being witnesses to them. But make up your mind not to worry beforehand how you will defend yourselves. For I will give you words and wisdom that none of your adversaries will be able to resist or contradict." Luke 21:12-15

5. **Jesus Acknowledges In Heaven To Our Father:** "Whoever acknowledges me before men, I will also acknowledge him before my Father in heaven." Matthew 10:32

6. **Jesus Acknowledges Before God's Angels:** "I tell you, whoever acknowledges me before men, the Son of Man will also acknowledge him before the angels of God." Luke 12:8

7. **When Hated, Excluded, Insulted and Rejected, One Is Blessed:** "Blessed are you when men hate you, when they exclude you and insult you and reject your name as evil, because of the Son of Man." Luke 6:22

Day 1: _____

_____
_____
_____
_____
_____
_____
_____
_____
_____
_____
_____

Day 2: _____

_____
_____
_____
_____
_____
_____
_____
_____
_____
_____
_____

Day 3: _____

_____
_____
_____
_____
_____
_____
_____
_____
_____
_____
_____

Words Of Wisdom: read a chapter from the Book of Proverbs corresponding with today's date (if today is the seventh, read chapter seven from the Book of Proverbs.)

Inasmuch as you have done it unto the least of these my brothers, you have done it unto me.
Matthew 25:40

Day 4: _____
_____
_____
_____
_____
_____
_____
_____
_____
_____

Day 5: _____
_____
_____
_____
_____
_____
_____
_____
_____
_____

Day 6: _____
_____
_____
_____
_____
_____
_____
_____
_____
_____

Day 7: _____
_____
_____
_____
_____
_____
_____
_____
_____
_____

Prayer Needs/Requests & How God Responded: _____

_____

_____

_____

_____

_____

_____

_____

_____

_____

_____

_____

_____

_____

Notes From This Week's Fellowship/Teaching: _____

_____

_____

_____

_____

_____

_____

_____

_____

_____

_____

_____

_____

_____

_____

_____

_____

_____

_____

_____

_____

_____

_____

Personal Accountability Checklist: (if in a group, have someone else check you)

☐ I completed the character or command promise study.
☐ I read a chapter from the Book Of Proverbs each day.
☐ I journaled each day.

Lesson 41: The Commandment To Take Seriously Christ's Message

1. **Repent And Believe His Good News:** " 'The time has come', he said. 'The kingdom of God is near. Repent and believe the good news.' " Mark 1:15

2. **Believe That You Have Received:** "Therefore I tell you, whatever you ask for in prayer, believe that you have received it, and it will be yours." Mark 11:24

3. **Trust In Christ Whom God Sent For You:** "Jesus answered, 'The work of God is this: to believe in the one he has sent.' " John 6:29

4. **Believe Christ Because Of His Work:** "Do not believe me unless I do what my Father does. But if I do it, even though you do not believe me, believe the miracles, that you may know and understand that the Father is in me, and I in the Father." John 10:37-38

5. **Trust In Christ In Order To Become God's Sons:** "Put your trust in the light while you have it, so that you may become sons of light." John 12:36

6. **Don't Be Troubled, Trust God And Christ:** "Do not let your hearts be troubled. Trust in God: trust also in me." John 14:1

7. **Believe That Jesus And The Father Are Unified:** "Believe me when I say that I am in the Father and the Father is in me; or at least believe on the evidence of the miracles themselves." John 14:11

Promises Of Jesus' Steadfast Presence

1. **When Obeying The Commission Jesus Is With Us:** "…and teaching them to obey everything I have commanded you. And surely I am with you always, to the very end of the age." Matthew 28:20

2. **Jesus Joins Those Gathered In His Name:** "For where two or three come together in my name, there am I with them." Matthew 18:20

3. **Jesus Comes To Us, We Are Not Orphans:** "I will not leave you as orphans; I will come to you." John 14:18

4. **Jesus, Our Father And The Believer Are Unified:** "On that day you will realize that I am in my Father, and you are in me, and I am in you." John 14:20

5. **Jesus Goes Away And Will Return To Us:** "You heard me say, 'I am going away and I am coming back to you.' If you loved me, you would be glad that I am going to the Father, for the Father is greater than I." John 14:28

6. **Jesus Reveals Himself To The Obedient:** "Whoever has my commands and obeys them, he is the one who loves me. He who loves me will be loved by my Father, and I too will love him and show myself to him." John 14:21

7. **Jesus And Our Father Make Their Home With The Obedient:** "Jesus replied, 'If anyone loves me, he will obey my teaching. My Father will love him, and we will come to him and make our home with him.' " John 14:23

Day 1: _____

_____

_____

_____

_____

_____

_____

_____

_____

_____

_____

_____

Day 2: _____

_____

_____

_____

_____

_____

_____

_____

_____

_____

_____

_____

Day 3: _____

_____

_____

_____

_____

_____

_____

_____

_____

_____

_____

_____

 Words Of Wisdom: read a chapter from the Book of Proverbs corresponding with today's date (if today is the seventh, read chapter seven from the Book of Proverbs.)

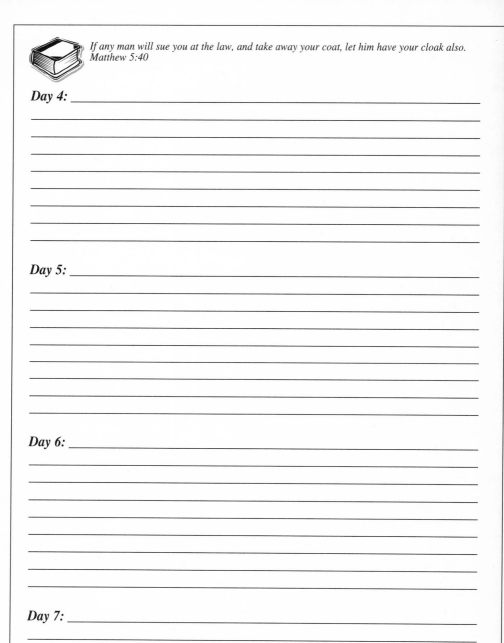

If any man will sue you at the law, and take away your coat, let him have your cloak also.
Matthew 5:40

Day 4: _____

_____
_____
_____
_____
_____
_____
_____
_____

Day 5: _____

_____
_____
_____
_____
_____
_____
_____
_____

Day 6: _____

_____
_____
_____
_____
_____
_____
_____
_____

Day 7: _____

_____
_____
_____
_____
_____
_____
_____
_____

Prayer Needs/Requests & How God Responded: _____

_____

_____

_____

_____

_____

_____

_____

_____

_____

_____

_____

_____

_____

_____

_____

Notes From This Week's Fellowship/Teaching: _____

_____

_____

_____

_____

_____

_____

_____

_____

_____

_____

_____

_____

_____

_____

_____

_____

_____

_____

_____

_____

_____

_____

_____

_____

_____

_____

_____

_____

_____

_____

Personal Accountability Checklist: (if in a group, have someone else check you)

☐ I completed the character or command promise study.
☐ I read a chapter from the Book Of Proverbs each day.
☐ I journaled each day.

Lesson 42: The Commandment To Be A Humble Servant

1. **Take His Yoke To Find Your Rest For Your Soul:** "Take my yoke upon you and learn from me, for I am gentle and humble in heart, and you will find rest for your souls." Matthew 11:29

2. **Serve, Do Not Exercise Authority:** "Jesus called them together and said, 'You know that the rulers of the Gentiles lord it over them, and their high officials exercise authority over them. Not so with you. Instead, whoever wants to become great among you must be your servant.' " Matthew 20:25-26

3. **Call Leaders Brother or Sister:** "But you are not to be called 'Rabbi,' for you have only one Master and you are all brothers." Matthew 23:8

4. **A Slave Of All Serves Everyone:** "Not so with you. Instead, whoever wants to become great among you must be your servant, and whoever wants to be first must be slave of all." Mark 10:43-44

5. **Rejoice Because You Are God's Child, Not For Your Ministry:** "However, do not rejoice that the spirits submit to you, but rejoice that your names are written in heaven." Luke 10:20

6. **When Honored, Sit In The Lowest Place:** "When someone invites you to a wedding feast, do not take the place of honor, for a person more distinguished than you may have been invited. If so, the host who invited both of you will come and say to you, 'Give this man your seat.' Then, humiliated, you will have to take the least important place. But when you are invited, take the lowest place, so that when your host comes, he will say to you. 'Friend, move up to a better place.' Then you will be honored in the presence of all your fellow guests. For everyone who exalts himself will be humbled, and he who humbles himself will be exalted." Luke 14:8-11

7. **Accept No Praise, Simply Do Your Duty:** "So you also, when you have done everything you were told to do, should say, 'We are unworthy servants; we have only done our duty.' " Luke 17:10

Promises To The Humble, Lowly, Kind And Pure Hearted

1. **The Kingdom Of Heaven For The Poor In Spirit:** "Blessed are the poor in spirit, for theirs is the kingdom of heaven." Matthew 5:3

2. **God's Comfort For The Mourners:** "Blessed are those who mourn, for they will be comforted." Matthew 5:4

3. **The Earth Inherited By The Meek:** "Blessed are the meek, for they will inherit the earth." Matthew 5:5

4. **Filled With Righteousness Are The Hungry:** "Blessed are those who hunger and thirst for righteousness, for they will be filled." Matthew 5:6

5. **Mercy Will Be Shown To The Merciful:** "Blessed are the merciful, for they will be shown mercy." Matthew 5:7

6. **Sons Of God Are Those That Make Peace:** "Blessed are the peacemakers, for they will be called sons of God." Matthew 5:9

7. **Those Who See God Are Pure In Heart:** "Blessed are the pure in heart, for they will see God." Matthew 5:8

Day 1: _____
_____
_____
_____
_____
_____
_____
_____
_____
_____
_____
_____

Day 2: _____
_____
_____
_____
_____
_____
_____
_____
_____
_____
_____
_____
_____
_____

Day 3: _____
_____
_____
_____
_____
_____
_____
_____
_____
_____
_____
_____
_____
_____

Words Of Wisdom: read a chapter from the Book of Proverbs corresponding with today's date (if today is the seventh, read chapter seven from the Book of Proverbs.)

By this will all men know that you are my disciples, if you have love one to another.
John 13:35

Day 4: _____
_____
_____
_____
_____
_____
_____
_____
_____

Day 5: _____
_____
_____
_____
_____
_____
_____
_____
_____

Day 6: _____
_____
_____
_____
_____
_____
_____
_____
_____

Day 7: _____
_____
_____
_____
_____
_____
_____
_____

Prayer Needs/Requests & How God Responded: _____

_____

_____

_____

_____

_____

_____

_____

_____

_____

_____

_____

_____

_____

_____

_____

_____

_____

Notes From This Week's Fellowship/Teaching: _____

_____

_____

_____

_____

_____

_____

_____

_____

_____

_____

_____

_____

_____

_____

_____

_____

_____

_____

_____

_____

_____

_____

_____

_____

_____

Personal Accountability Checklist: (if in a group, have someone else check you)

- ☐ I completed the character or command promise study.
- ☐ I read a chapter from the Book Of Proverbs each day.
- ☐ I journaled each day.

Lesson 43: The Commandment To Remain In Christ's Word

1. Recognize False Prophets: "Watch out for false prophets. They come to you in sheep's clothing, but inwardly they are ferocious wolves. By their fruit you will recognize them. Do people pick grapes from thornbushes, or grapes from thistles? Likewise every good tree bears good fruit, but a bad tree bears bad fruit." Matthew 7:15-17

2. **Recognize Yeast (false teachings and doctrines):** " 'Be careful,' Jesus said to them. 'Be on your guard against the yeast of the Pharisees and Sadducees.' " Matthew 16:6

3. **Evaluate Carefully What You Hear:** " 'Consider carefully what you hear,' he continued, 'With the measure you use, it will be measured to you – and even more.' " Mark 4:24

4. **Determine To Retain What You Hear:** "Therefore consider carefully how you listen. Whoever has will be given more; whoever does not have, even what he thinks he has will be taken from him." Luke 8:18

5. **When Our King Speaks, Really Listen:** "Listen carefully to what I am about to tell you: The son of Man is going to be betrayed into the hands of men." Luke 9:44

6. **Diligently Study The Scripture About Christ:** "You diligently study the Scriptures because you think that by them you possess eternal life. These are the Scriptures that testify about me." John 5:39

7. **Expect Others To Treat You Like Christ Was Treated:** "Remember the words I spoke to you: 'No servant is greater than his master.' If they persecuted me, they will persecute you also. If they obeyed my teaching they will obey yours also." John 15:20

Promises For One Who Obeys His Commands

1. **Those Called Great In The Kingdom Practice And Teach His Commands:** "Anyone who breaks one of the least of these commandments and teaches others to do the same will be called least in the kingdom of heaven, but whoever practices and teaches these commands will be called great in the kingdom of heaven." Matthew 5:19

2. **He Will Build His House Wisely:** "Therefore everyone who hears these words of mine and puts them into practice is like a wise man who built his house on the rock. The rain came down, the streams rose, and the winds blew and beat against that house; yet it did not fall, because it had its foundation on the rock." Matthew 7:24-25

3. **He Will Be Loved By Jesus And Our Father:** "Whoever has my commands and obeys them, he is the one who loves me. He who loves me will be loved by my Father, and I too will love him and show myself to him." John 14:21

4. **The Obedient Become The Home Of Our Father And Jesus:** "Jesus replied, 'If anyone loves me, he will obey my teaching. My Father will love him, and we will come to him and make our home with him.' " John 14:23

5. **The Obedient Remain In Jesus' Love:** "If you obey my commands, you will remain in my love, just as I have obeyed my Father's commands and remain in his love." John 15:10

6. **Will Be A Friend To Jesus:** "You are my friends if you do what I command." John 15:14

7. **Will Have The Right To Enter The Gates And Tree Of Life:** "Blessed are those who wash their robes, that they may have the right to the tree of life and may go through the gates into the city." Revelation 22:14

Day 1: _____
_____
_____
_____
_____
_____
_____
_____
_____
_____
_____
_____

Day 2: _____
_____
_____
_____
_____
_____
_____
_____
_____
_____
_____
_____

Day 3: _____
_____
_____
_____
_____
_____
_____
_____
_____
_____
_____
_____
_____

 Words Of Wisdom: read a chapter from the Book of Proverbs corresponding with today's date (if today is the seventh, read chapter seven from the Book of Proverbs.)

If you do whatever I command you, you are my friends. John 15:14

Day 4: _____

_____
_____
_____
_____
_____
_____
_____
_____
_____

Day 5: _____

_____
_____
_____
_____
_____
_____
_____
_____
_____

Day 6: _____

_____
_____
_____
_____
_____
_____
_____
_____

Day 7: _____

_____
_____
_____
_____
_____
_____
_____
_____

Prayer Needs/Requests & How God Responded: _____

_____
_____
_____
_____
_____
_____
_____
_____
_____
_____
_____
_____

Notes From This Week's Fellowship/Teaching: _____

_____
_____
_____
_____
_____
_____
_____
_____
_____
_____
_____
_____
_____
_____
_____
_____
_____
_____
_____
_____
_____
_____
_____

Personal Accountability Checklist: (if in a group, have someone else check you)
- ☐ I completed the character or command promise study.
- ☐ I read a chapter from the Book Of Proverbs each day.
- ☐ I journaled each day.

Lesson 44: The Commandment To Daily Live Like Christ

1. **Fulfill All Righteousness And Obey All His Commands:** "Jesus replied, 'Let it be so now; it is proper for us to do this to fulfill all righteousness.' Then John consented." Matthew 3:15 "Therefore go and make disciples of all nations, baptizing them in the name of the Father and the Son and of the Holy Spirit, and teaching them to obey everything I have commanded you. And surely I am with you always, to the very end of the age." Matthew 28:19-20

2. **Become Gentle And Humble In Heart Through Christ's Yoke**: "Take my yoke upon you and learn from me, for I am gentle and humble in heart, and you will find rest for your souls." Matthew 11:29

3. **Deny Yourself, Take Up Your Cross Daily And Follow Jesus:** "Then he said to them all: 'If anyone would come after me, he must deny himself and take up his cross daily and follow me.' " Luke 9:23

4. **Remember How Christ Lived And Died:** "After taking the cup, he gave thanks and said, 'Take this and divide it among you. For I tell you I will not drink again of the fruit of the vine until the kingdom of God comes.' And he took bread, gave thanks and broke it, and gave it to them, saying, 'This is my body given for you; do this in remembrance of me.' " Luke 22:17-19

5. **Our Father Honors Those Who Live Like Jesus:** "Whoever serves me must follow me; and where I am, my servant also will be. My Father will honor the one who serves me." John 12:26

6. **Do As Christ Did:** "Now that I, your Lord and Teacher, have washed your feet, you also should wash one another's feet. I have set you an example that you should do as I have done for you." John 13:14-15

7. **Love Others With His Love That's In You:** "As the Father has loved me, so have I loved you. Now remain in my love." John 15:9

Promises For One Following Christ's Pattern

1. **Will Have The Light Of Life:** "When Jesus spoke again to the people, he said , 'I am the light of the world. Whoever follows me will never walk in darkness, but will have the light of life.' " John 8:12

2. **Will Be Given Eternal Life:** "My sheep listen to my voice; I know them, and they follow me. I give them eternal life, and they shall never perish; no one can snatch them out of my hand." John 10:27-28

3. **He Will Find His Life:** "Then Jesus said to his disciples, 'If anyone would come after me, he must deny himself and take up his cross and follow me. For whoever wants to save his life will lose it, but whoever loses his life for me will find it." Matthew 16:24, 25

4. **He Will Gain Heavenly Treasure:** "Jesus answered, 'If you want to be perfect, go, sell your possessions and give to the poor, and you will have treasure in heaven. Then come, follow me.' " Matthew 19:21

5. **Will Have One Hundred Fold Now:** "Peter said to him, 'We have left everything to follow you!' 'I tell you the truth,' Jesus replied, 'no one who has left home or brothers or sisters or mother or father or children or fields for me and the gospel will fail to receive a hundred times as much in this present age (homes, brothers, sisters, mothers, children and fields – and with them, persecutions) and in the age to come, eternal life.' " Mark 10:28-30

6. **Will Be Made Fishers Of Men:** " 'Come follow me,' Jesus said, 'and I will make you fishers of men.' " Matthew 4:19

7. **Will Be Honored By Our Father:** "Whoever serves me must follow me; and where I am, my servant also will be. My Father will honor the one who serves me." John 12:26

Day 1: _____
_____
_____
_____
_____
_____
_____
_____
_____
_____
_____
_____
_____
_____

Day 2: _____
_____
_____
_____
_____
_____
_____
_____
_____
_____
_____
_____
_____
_____

Day 3: _____
_____
_____
_____
_____
_____
_____
_____
_____
_____
_____
_____
_____
_____
_____

 Words Of Wisdom: read a chapter from the Book of Proverbs corresponding with today's date (if today is the seventh, read chapter seven from the Book of Proverbs.)

Have salt in yourselves, and have peace with one another. Mark 9:50

Day 4: _____
_____
_____
_____
_____
_____
_____
_____
_____
_____

Day 5: _____
_____
_____
_____
_____
_____
_____
_____
_____
_____

Day 6: _____
_____
_____
_____
_____
_____
_____
_____
_____
_____

Day 7: _____
_____
_____
_____
_____
_____
_____
_____
_____

Prayer Needs/Requests & How God Responded: _____

_____

_____

_____

_____

_____

_____

_____

_____

_____

_____

_____

_____

_____

Notes From This Week's Fellowship/Teaching: _____

_____

_____

_____

_____

_____

_____

_____

_____

_____

_____

_____

_____

_____

_____

_____

_____

_____

_____

_____

_____

_____

_____

_____

_____

Personal Accountability Checklist: (if in a group, have someone else check you)

☐   I completed the character or command promise study.
☐   I read a chapter from the Book Of Proverbs each day.
☐   I journaled each day.

Lesson 45: The Commandment To Be Faithful In Prayer

1. **Secret Prayer In Jesus' Name Brings Our Father's Rewards:** "But when you pray, go into your room, close the door and pray to your Father who is unseen. Then your Father, who sees what is done in secret, will reward you." Matthew 6:6 "Until now you have not asked for anything in my name. Ask and you will receive and your joy will be complete" John 16:24

2. **Our Father Knows, So Don't Babble:** "And when you pray, do not keep on babbling like pagans, for they think they will be heard because of their many words. Do not be like them, for your Father knows what you need before you ask him." Matthew 6:7-8

3. **Carefully Follow Christ's Example In Your Prayers:** "This, then, is how you should pray: 'Our Father in heaven, hallowed be your name, your kingdom come, your will be done on earth as it is in heaven. Give us today our daily bread. Forgive us our debts, as we also have forgiven our debtors. And lead us not into temptation, but deliver us from the evil one." Matthew 6:9-13

4. **Pray For Those Who Mistreat, Bless Those Who Curse:** "Bless those who curse you, pray for those who mistreat you." Luke 6:28

5. **Pray For More Sent Out Workers:** "He told them, 'The harvest is plentiful, but the workers are few. Ask the Lord of the harvest, therefore, to send out workers into his harvest field.' " Luke 10:2

6. **To Escape And Stand, Always Watch And Pray:** "Be always on the watch, and pray that you may be able to escape all that is about to happen, and that you may be able to stand before the Son Of Man." Luke 21:36

7. **Pray To Prevent Your Personal Sin:** " 'Why are you sleeping?' he asked them. 'Get up and pray so that you will not fall into temptation.' " Luke 22:46

Promises Of Prayer Results

1. **He Who Asks, Seeks And Knocks…Receives:** "For everyone who asks receives, he who seeks finds; and to him who knocks, the door will be opened." Matthew 7:8

2. **Our Father Gives Good Gifts To Those Who Ask:** "If you, then, though you are evil, know how to give good gifts to your children, how much more will your Father in heaven give good gifts to those who ask him!" Matthew 7:11

3. **If You Believe, You Will Receive:** "If you believe, you will receive whatever you ask for in prayer." Matthew 21:22

4. **Unity In God's Will Brings Results:** "Again, I tell you that if two of you on earth agree about anything you ask for, it will be done for you by my Father in heaven. " Matthew 18:19

5. **Results Come From Boldness:** "I tell you, though he will not get up and give him the bread because he is his friend, yet because of the man's boldness he will get up and give him as much as he needs." Luke 11:8

6. **Results Come For Those Who Continue To Pray:** "And will not God bring about justice for his chosen ones, who cry out to him day and night? Will he keep putting them off? I tell you, he will see that they get justice, and quickly. However, when the Son of Man comes, will he find faith on the earth?" Luke 18: 7-8

7. **Continual Obedience To Jesus' Words Brings Results:** "If you remain in me and my words remain in you, ask whatever you wish, and it will be given you." John 15:7

Day 1: _____

_____

_____

_____

_____

_____

_____

_____

_____

_____

_____

_____

_____

Day 2: _____

_____

_____

_____

_____

_____

_____

_____

_____

_____

_____

_____

_____

Day 3: _____

_____

_____

_____

_____

_____

_____

_____

_____

_____

_____

_____

_____

 Words Of Wisdom: read a chapter from the Book of Proverbs corresponding with today's date (if today is the seventh, read chapter seven from the Book of Proverbs.)

For I came down from heaven, not to do my will, but the will of him that sent me. And this is the Father's will which sent me, that all of which he has given me, I should lose nothing, but raise it up again at the last day. And that every one which sees the Son, and believes on him, may have everlasting life: and I will raise him up at the last day. John 6:38-40.

Day 4: _____

_____

_____

_____

_____

_____

_____

_____

_____

_____

Day 5: _____

_____

_____

_____

_____

_____

_____

_____

_____

_____

Day 6: _____

_____

_____

_____

_____

_____

_____

_____

_____

_____

Day 7: _____

_____

_____

_____

_____

_____

_____

_____

_____

_____

Prayer Needs/Requests & How God Responded: _____

_____
_____
_____
_____
_____
_____
_____
_____
_____
_____
_____
_____
_____

Notes From This Week's Fellowship/Teaching: _____

_____
_____
_____
_____
_____
_____
_____
_____
_____
_____
_____
_____
_____
_____
_____
_____
_____
_____
_____
_____
_____
_____
_____
_____

Personal Accountability Checklist: (if in a group, have someone else check you)

☐ I completed the character or command promise study.
☐ I read a chapter from the Book Of Proverbs each day.
☐ I journaled each day.

Week 46: The Commandment To Store Up Heavenly Treasures

1. **Give And Lend:** "Give to the one who asks you, and do not turn away from the one who wants to borrow from you." Matthew 5:42
2. **Store Up Heavenly Treasure, Not Earthly:** "Do not store up for yourselves treasures on earth, where moth and rust destroy, and where thieves break in and steal. But store up for yourselves treasures in heaven, where moth and rust do not destroy, and where thieves do not break in and steal." Matthew 6:19-20
3. **Practice Tithing, Justice, Mercy And Faithfulness:** "Woe to you, teachers of the law and Pharisees, you hypocrites! You give a tenth of your spices – mint, dill and cumin. But you have neglected the more important matters of the law – justice, mercy and faithfulness. You should have practiced the latter, without neglecting the former." Matthew 23:23
4. **Give To The Poor, To Become Clean:** "But give what is inside the dish to the poor, and everything will be clean for you." Luke 11:41
5. **Guard Yourselves Against All Kinds Of Greed:** "Then he said to them, 'Watch out! Be on your guard against all kinds of greed; a man's life does not consist in the abundance of his possessions.' " Luke 12:15
6. **Invite The Poor, Crippled, Lame And Blind For Resurrection Repayment:** "Then Jesus said to his host, 'When you give a luncheon or dinner, do not invite your friends, your brothers or relatives, or your rich neighbors; if you do, they may invite you back and so you will be repaid. But when you give a banquet, invite the poor, the crippled, the lame, the blind, and you will be blessed. Although they cannot repay you, you will be repaid at the resurrection of the righteous.' " Luke 14:12-13
7. **Use Wealth To Gain Eternal Friendships:** "I tell you, use worldly wealth to gain friends for yourselves, so that when it is gone, you will be welcomed into eternal dwellings." Luke 16:9

Promises For The Use Of Jesus' Name

1. **To Bring Glory To The Father, Ask In Jesus' Name:** "And I will do whatever you ask in my name, so that the Son may bring glory to the Father." John 14:13
2. **Ask For Anything In Jesus' Name:** "You may ask me for anything in my name, and I will do it." John 14:14
3. **To Produce Lasting Fruit Ask Anything In Jesus' Name:** "You did not choose me, but I chose you and appointed you to go and bear fruit – fruit that will last. Then the Father will give you whatever you ask in my name." John 15:16
4. **Our Father Will Give Whatever Is Asked In Jesus' Name:** "In that day you will no longer ask me anything. I tell you the truth, my Father will give you whatever you ask in my name." John 16:23
5. **To Receive Complete Joy, Ask In Jesus' Name:** "Until now you have not asked for anything in my name. Ask and you will receive, and your joy will be complete." John 16:24
6. **In That Day You Will Ask Our Father In Jesus' Name:** "In that day you will ask in my name. I am not saying that I will ask the Father on your behalf. No, the Father himself loves you because you have loved me and have believed that I came from God." John 16:26-27
7. **Believers Are Empowered:** "And these signs will accompany those who believe: In my name they will drive out demons; they will speak in new tongues; they will pick up snakes with their hands; and when they drink deadly poison, it will not hurt them at all; they will place their hands on sick people, and they will get well." Mark 16:17-18

Day 1: _____

_____

_____

_____

_____

_____

_____

_____

_____

_____

_____

Day 2: _____

_____

_____

_____

_____

_____

_____

_____

_____

_____

_____

_____

Day 3: _____

_____

_____

_____

_____

_____

_____

_____

_____

_____

_____

_____

Words Of Wisdom: read a chapter from the Book of Proverbs corresponding with today's date (if today is the seventh, read chapter seven from the Book of Proverbs.)

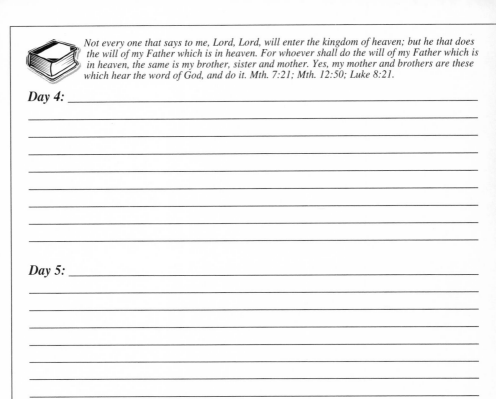

Not every one that says to me, Lord, Lord, will enter the kingdom of heaven; but he that does the will of my Father which is in heaven. For whoever shall do the will of my Father which is in heaven, the same is my brother, sister and mother. Yes, my mother and brothers are these which hear the word of God, and do it. Mth. 7:21; Mth. 12:50; Luke 8:21.

Day 4: _____

_____
_____
_____
_____
_____
_____
_____
_____
_____

Day 5: _____

_____
_____
_____
_____
_____
_____
_____
_____
_____

Day 6: _____

_____
_____
_____
_____
_____
_____
_____
_____
_____

Day 7: _____

_____
_____
_____
_____
_____
_____
_____
_____

Prayer Needs/Requests & How God Responded: _____

_____

_____

_____

_____

_____

_____

_____

_____

_____

_____

_____

_____

_____

_____

Notes From This Week's Fellowship/Teaching: _____

_____

_____

_____

_____

_____

_____

_____

_____

_____

_____

_____

_____

_____

_____

_____

_____

_____

_____

_____

_____

_____

_____

_____

_____

Personal Accountability Checklist: (if in a group, have someone else check you)

- ☐ I completed the character or command promise study.
- ☐ I read a chapter from the Book Of Proverbs each day.
- ☐ I journaled each day.

Lesson 47: The Commandment To Remain In Christ

1. **Make Your Own Tree Good To Receive Good Fruit:** "Make a tree good and its fruit will be good, or make a tree bad and its fruit will be bad, for a tree is recognized by its fruit." Matthew 12:33

2. **Clean The Inside First:** "Blind Pharisee! First clean the inside of the cup and dish, and then the outside also will be clean." Matthew 23:26

3. **Be Different, Yet Inoffensive:** "Salt is good, but if it loses its saltiness, how can you make it salty again? Have salt in yourselves, and be at peace with each other." Mark 9:50

4. **Rejoice That Your Name Is In Heaven:** "However, do not rejoice that the spirits submit to you, but rejoice that your names are written in heaven." Luke 10:20

5. **Spiritual Birth Is Essential:** "You should not be surprised at my saying, 'You must be born again.' " John 3:7

6. **Work For Food That Lasts Eternally:** "Do not work for food that spoils, but for food that endures to eternal life, which the Son of Man will give you. On him God the Father has placed his seal of approval." John 6:27

7. **To Produce Spiritual Fruit, Continue To Obey Christ:** "Remain in me, and I will remain in you. No branch can bear fruit by itself; it must remain in the vine. Neither can you bear fruit unless you remain in me." John 15:4

Promises Of Being Raised From The Dead

1. **Pay Day Of The Righteous At The Resurrection:** "But when you give a banquet, invite the poor, the crippled, the lame, the blind, and you will be blessed. Although they cannot repay you, you will be repaid at the resurrection of the righteous." Luke 14:13-14

2. **God's Children Can No Longer Die:** "But those who are considered worthy of taking part in that age and in the resurrection from the dead will neither marry nor be given in marriage, and they can no longer die; for they are like the angels. They are God's children, since they are children of the resurrection." Luke 20:35-36

3. **All Are Alive Unto God:** "But in the account of the bush, even Moses showed that the dead rise, for he calls the Lord 'the God of Abraham, and the God of Isaac, and the God of Jacob. He is not the God of the dead, but of the living, for to him all are alive.' " Luke 20:37-38

4. **Jesus Raises The Dead Just As Our Father Does:** "For just as the Father raises the dead and gives them life, even so the Son gives life to whom he is pleased to give it." John 5:21

5. **At Jesus' Voice All Will Be Raised:** "Do not be amazed at this, for a time is coming when all who are in their graves will hear his voice and come out – those who have done good will rise to live, and those who have done evil will rise to be condemned." John 5:28-29

6. **Jesus Will Raise Believers To Eternal Life At The Last Day:** "For my Father's will is that everyone who looks to the Son and believes in him shall have eternal life, and I will raise him up at the last day." John 6:40

7. **Whoever Believes In Jesus Will Never Die:** "Jesus said to her, 'I am the resurrection and the life. He who believes in me will live, even though he dies; and whoever lives and believes in me will never die. Do you believe this?' " John 11: 25-26

Day 1: _____

_____

_____

_____

_____

_____

_____

_____

_____

_____

_____

_____

_____

_____

Day 2: _____

_____

_____

_____

_____

_____

_____

_____

_____

_____

_____

_____

_____

Day 3: _____

_____

_____

_____

_____

_____

_____

_____

_____

_____

_____

_____

_____

_____

 Words Of Wisdom: read a chapter from the Book of Proverbs corresponding with today's date (if today is the seventh, read chapter seven from the Book of Proverbs.)

He that enters in by the door is the shepherd of the sheep, and the sheep hear his voice: and he calls his sheep by name, and leads them out. He goes before them, and the sheep follow him: for they know his voice. And a stranger they will not follow, but will flee from him: for they do not know the voice of strangers. John 10:2-5.

Day 4: _____

_____
_____
_____
_____
_____
_____
_____
_____
_____

Day 5: _____

_____
_____
_____
_____
_____
_____
_____
_____
_____

Day 6: _____

_____
_____
_____
_____
_____
_____
_____
_____
_____

Day 7: _____

_____
_____
_____
_____
_____
_____
_____
_____
_____

Prayer Needs/Requests & How God Responded: _____

_____

_____

_____

_____

_____

_____

_____

_____

_____

_____

_____

_____

_____

_____

Notes From This Week's Fellowship/Teaching: _____

_____

_____

_____

_____

_____

_____

_____

_____

_____

_____

_____

_____

_____

_____

_____

_____

_____

_____

_____

_____

_____

_____

Personal Accountability Checklist: (if in a group, have someone else check you)

☐ I completed the character or command promise study.
☐ I read a chapter from the Book Of Proverbs each day.
☐ I journaled each day.

Lesson 48: The Commandment To Be Ready For Christ's Coming

1. **Expect And Watch For Many Deceivers:** "Jesus said to them, 'Watch out that no one deceives you. Many will come in my name, claiming, "I am he," and will deceive many.' " Mark 13:5-6

2. **Watch For Christ's Sudden Coming:** "Therefore keep watch because you do not know when the owner of the house will come back – whether in the evening, or at midnight, or when the rooster crows, or at dawn. If he comes suddenly, do not let him find you sleeping. What I say to you, I say to everyone: Watch!" Mark 13:35-37

3. **Be Ready For Christ's Return:** "Be dressed ready for service and keep your lamps burning, like men waiting for their master to return from a wedding banquet, so that when he comes and knocks they can immediately open the door for him." Luke 12:35-36

4. **You Never Know When Christ Will Come:** "You also must be ready, because the Son of Man will come at an hour when you do not expect him." Luke 12:40

5. **Don't Treasure Anything Of This Earth:** "On that day no one who is on the roof of his house, with his goods inside, should go down to get them. Likewise, no one in the field should go back for anything. Remember Lot's wife!" Luke 17:31-32

6. **Watch Your Hearts And Your Feelings To Be Ready For His Coming:** "Be careful, or your hearts will be weighted down with dissipation, drunkenness and the anxieties of life, and that day will close on you unexpectedly like a trap." Luke 21:34

7. **Hold On, Wake Up, Make Stronger, Finish His Assignments:** "Only hold on to what you have until I come" Revelation 2:25 "Wake up! Strengthen what remains and is about to die, for I have not found your deeds complete in the sight of my God. Remember, therefore, what you have received and heard; obey it, and repent. But if you do not wake up, I will come like a thief, and you will not know at what time I will come to you." Revelation 3:2-3

Promises Of Christ's Glorious Worldwide Coming

1. **Jesus Comes With Power And Great Glory:** "At that time they will see the Son of Man coming in a cloud with power and great glory. When these things begin to take place, stand up and lift up your heads, because your redemption is drawing near." Luke 21:27-28

2. **Jesus' Coming Will Be As Visible As Lightning:** "For as lightning that comes from the east is visible even in the west, so will be the coming of the Son of Man." Matthew 24:27

3. **His Angels Will Gather His Elect From The Ends Of Heaven:** "And he will send his angels with a loud trumpet call, and they will gather his elect from the four winds, from one end of the heavens to the other." Matthew 24:31

4. **Jesus Comes To Take His Own To Be With Him:** "And if I go and prepare a place for you, I will come back and take you to be with me that you also may be where I am." John 14:3

5. **Ready, Watchful Servants Will Be Waited Upon By Jesus:** "It will be good for those servants whose master finds them watching when he comes. I tell you the truth, he will dress himself to serve, will have them recline at the table and will come and wait on them. It will be good for those servants whose master finds them ready, even if he comes in the second or third watch of the night." Luke 12:37-38

6. **The Faithful Wise Servant Will Be Put In Charge Of All Jesus' Possessions:** "The Lord answered, 'Who then is the faithful and wise manager, whom the master puts in charge of his servants to give them their food allowance at the proper time? It will be good for that servant whom the master finds doing so when he returns. I tell you the truth, he will put him in charge of all his possessions.' " Luke 12:43-44

7. **Jesus Will Judge From His Heavenly Glory Throne:** "When the Son of Man comes in his glory, and all the angels with him, he will sit on his throne in heavenly glory." Matthew 25:31

Day 1: _____

_____

_____

_____

_____

_____

_____

_____

_____

_____

_____

_____

_____

Day 2: _____

_____

_____

_____

_____

_____

_____

_____

_____

_____

_____

_____

_____

Day 3: _____

_____

_____

_____

_____

_____

_____

_____

_____

_____

_____

_____

_____

_____

 Words Of Wisdom: read a chapter from the Book of Proverbs corresponding with today's date (if today is the seventh, read chapter seven from the Book of Proverbs.)

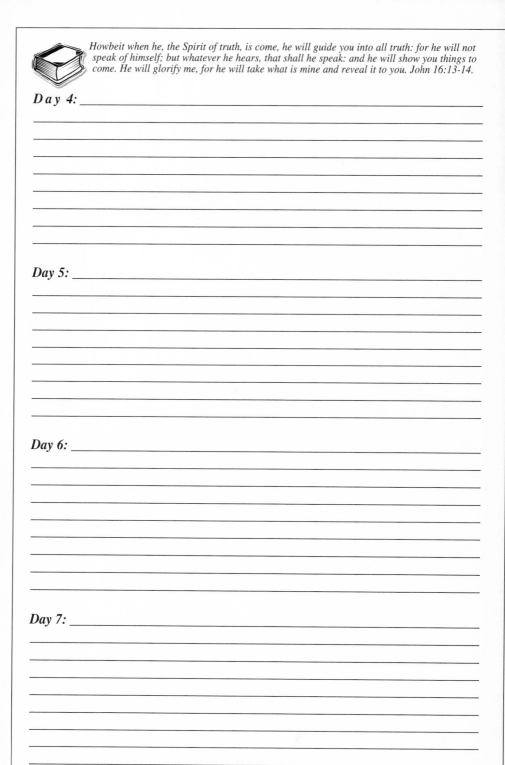

Howbeit when he, the Spirit of truth, is come, he will guide you into all truth: for he will not speak of himself; but whatever he hears, that shall he speak: and he will show you things to come. He will glorify me, for he will take what is mine and reveal it to you. John 16:13-14.

Day 4: _____

_____

_____

_____

_____

_____

_____

_____

_____

_____

Day 5: _____

_____

_____

_____

_____

_____

_____

_____

_____

_____

Day 6: _____

_____

_____

_____

_____

_____

_____

_____

_____

_____

Day 7: _____

_____

_____

_____

_____

_____

_____

_____

_____

_____

Prayer Needs/Requests & How God Responded: _____

_____

_____

_____

_____

_____

_____

_____

_____

_____

_____

_____

_____

_____

_____

Notes From This Week's Fellowship/Teaching: _____

_____

_____

_____

_____

_____

_____

_____

_____

_____

_____

_____

_____

_____

_____

_____

_____

_____

_____

_____

_____

_____

_____

_____

_____

Personal Accountability Checklist: (if in a group, have someone else check you)

- ☐ I completed the character or command promise study.
- ☐ I read a chapter from the Book Of Proverbs each day.
- ☐ I journaled each day.

Lesson 49: The Commandment Not To Fear But Live In Faith

1. **Don't Worry About Essentials:** "Therefore I tell you, do not worry about your life, what you will eat or drink; or about your body, what you will wear. Is not life more important than clothes?" Matthew 6:25

2. **Take Courage, Jesus Is With Us:** "But Jesus immediately said to them: 'Take courage! It is I. Don't be afraid.' " Matthew 14:27

3. **Don't Fear Man Or The Devil, Fear God:** "Ignoring what they said, Jesus told the synagogue ruler, 'Don't be afraid; just believe.' " Mark 5:36 "I tell you, my friends, do not be afraid of those who kill the body and after that can do not more. But I will show you whom you should fear. Fear him who, after the killing of the body, has power to throw you into hell. Yes, I tell you, fear him." Luke 12:4-5

4. **Faith In God Can Remove Mountains:** " 'Have faith in God,' Jesus answered. 'I tell you the truth, if anyone says to this mountain, "Go, throw yourself into the sea," and does not doubt in his heart but believes that what he says will happen, it will be done for him.' " Mark 11:22

5. **Do Not Worry About Food And Drink:** "And do not set your heart on what you will eat or drink; do not worry about your body, what you will wear. Is not life more important than clothes?" Luke 12:29

6. **Do Not Let Your Hearts Be Troubled Or Afraid:** "Peace I leave with you; my peace I give you. I do not give to you as the world gives. Do not let your hearts be troubled and do not be afraid." John 14:27

7. **Stop Doubting, Believe In Jesus:** "Then he said to Thomas, 'Put your finger here; see my hands. Reach out your hand and put it into my side. Stop doubting and believe.' " John 20:27

Promises For The Use Of One's Belief In God

1. **Everything Is Possible For The Believer:** " 'If you can?' Said Jesus. 'Everything is possible for him who believes.' " Mark 9:23

2. **Nothing Will Be Impossible:** "He replied, 'Because you have so little faith. I tell you the truth, if you have faith as small as a mustard seed, you can say to this mountain, "Move from here to there" and it will move. Nothing will be impossible for you.' " Matthew 17:20

3. **Mustard Seed Size Faith Causes Uprooting And Planting:** "He replied, 'If you have faith as small as a mustard seed, you can say to this mulberry tree, "Be uprooted and planted in the sea," and it will obey you.' " Luke 17:6

4. **Faith In God With No Doubting Can Remove Mountains:** " 'Have faith in God,' Jesus answered. 'I tell you the truth, if anyone says to this mountain, "Go throw yourself into the sea," and does not doubt in his heart but believes that what he says will happen, it will be done for him.' " Mark 11:22-23

5. **Complete Faith Includes Belief Of Receiving:** "Therefore I tell you, whatever you ask for in prayer, believe that you have received it, and it will be yours." Mark 11:24

6. **To See The Glory Of God One Must Believe:** "...Did I not tell you that if you believed, you would see the glory of God?" John 11:40

7. **Greater Things Can Be Done By Faith:** "I tell you the truth, anyone who has faith in me will do what I have been doing. He will do even greater things than these, because I am going to the Father." John 14:12

Day 1: _____
_____
_____
_____
_____
_____
_____
_____
_____
_____
_____
_____

Day 2: _____
_____
_____
_____
_____
_____
_____
_____
_____
_____
_____
_____

Day 3: _____
_____
_____
_____
_____
_____
_____
_____
_____
_____
_____
_____

Words Of Wisdom: read a chapter from the Book of Proverbs corresponding with today's date (if today is the seventh, read chapter seven from the Book of Proverbs.)

Whoever comes to me, and hears my sayings, and does them, I will show you who he is like: He is like a man which built a house, and digged deep and laid the foundation on a rock: and when the flood arose, the stream beat violently upon that house, and could not shake it: for it was founded upon a rock. Luke 6:47-48.

Day 4: _____

_____
_____
_____
_____
_____
_____
_____
_____
_____

Day 5: _____

_____
_____
_____
_____
_____
_____
_____
_____
_____

Day 6: _____

_____
_____
_____
_____
_____
_____
_____
_____
_____

Day 7: _____

_____
_____
_____
_____
_____
_____
_____
_____
_____

Prayer Needs/Requests & How God Responded: _____

_____
_____
_____
_____
_____
_____
_____
_____
_____
_____
_____
_____

Notes From This Week's Fellowship/Teaching: _____

_____
_____
_____
_____
_____
_____
_____
_____
_____
_____
_____
_____
_____
_____
_____
_____
_____
_____
_____
_____
_____
_____
_____
_____
_____

Personal Accountability Checklist: (if in a group, have someone else check you)

- ☐ I completed the character or command promise study.
- ☐ I read a chapter from the Book Of Proverbs each day.
- ☐ I journaled each day.

Lesson 50: The Commandment To Serve God And Man

1. **Settle Matters With Your Opponent Quickly:** "Settle matters quickly with your adversary who is taking you to court. Do it while you are still with him on the way, or he may hand you over to the judge, and the judge may hand you over to the officer, and you may be thrown into prison." Matthew 5:25

2. **Walk Your Talk:** "But I tell you, do not swear at all; either by heaven, for it is God's throne; or by the earth, for it is his footstool; or by Jerusalem, for it is the city of the Great King. And do not swear by your head, for you cannot make even one hair white or black. Simply let your 'Yes' be 'Yes,' and your 'No, No'; anything beyond this comes from the evil one." Matthew 5:34-37

3. **Keep Your Agreements:** "…for this reason a man will leave his father and mother and be united to his wife, and the two will become one flesh? So they are no longer two, but one. Therefore what God has joined together, let man not separate." Matthew 19:5-6

4. **Don't Stop Other's Ministry Done In His Name:** " 'Do not stop him,' Jesus said. 'No one who does a miracle in my name can in the next moment say anything bad about me, for whoever is not against us is for us.' " Mark 9:39-40

5. **Give To All What Is Due Them:** "Then Jesus said to them, 'Give to Caesar what is Caesar's and to God what is God's.' " Mark 12:17

6. **Eat What Is Provided By Your Supporters:** "When you enter a town and are welcomed, eat what is set before you." Luke 10:8

7. **Waste Nothing:** "When they had all had enough to eat, he said to his disciples, 'Gather the pieces that are left over. Let nothing be wasted.' " John 6:12

Promises Of Eternal Rewards For Faithful Workers

1. **Great Rewards When Responding Correctly To Enemies:** "But love your enemies, do good to them, and lend to them without expecting to get anything back. Then your reward will be great, and you will be sons of the Most High, because he is kind to the ungrateful and wicked." Luke 6:35

2. **He Who Reaps Draws Wages:** "Even now the reaper draws his wages, even now he harvests the crop for eternal life, so that the sower and reaper may be glad together. " John 4:36

3. **A Prophet's Or Righteous Man's Rewards Received:** "Anyone who receives a prophet because he is a prophet will receive a prophet's reward, and anyone who receives a righteous man because he is a righteous man will receive a righteous man's reward." Matthew 10:41-42

4. **To Lose Life Is To Find It:** For the Son of Man is going to come in his Father's glory with his angels, and then he will reward each person according to what he has done." Matthew 16:27

5. **Even A Cup Of Cold Water Is Rewarded:** "And if anyone gives even a cup of cold water to one of these little ones because he is my disciple, I tell you the truth, he will certainly not lose his reward." Matthew 10:42

6. **Faithful Servants To Share In Authority And Happiness Of The Master:** "His master replied, 'Well done, good and faithful servant. You have been faithful with a few things; I will put you in charge of many things. Come and share your master's happiness!' " Matthew 25:21

7. **Good, Trustworthy Servants Will Receive More Authority:** " 'Well done, my good servant!' his master replied. 'Because you have been trustworthy in a very small matter, take charge of ten cities.' " Luke 19:17

Day 1: _____
_____
_____
_____
_____
_____
_____
_____
_____
_____
_____
_____
_____
_____
_____

Day 2: _____
_____
_____
_____
_____
_____
_____
_____
_____
_____
_____
_____
_____
_____
_____

Day 3: _____
_____
_____
_____
_____
_____
_____
_____
_____
_____
_____
_____
_____
_____
_____
_____

Words Of Wisdom: read a chapter from the Book of Proverbs corresponding with today's date (if today is the seventh, read chapter seven from the Book of Proverbs.)

Have faith in God, for truly I tell you, that whoever will say unto this mountain, Be removed, and be cast into the sea; and will not doubt in his heart, but shall believe that those things which he says will come to pass; he will have whatever he says. Therefore I tell you, the things you desire when you pray, believe that you receive them, and you will have them. Mark 11:22-24.

Day 4: _____
_____
_____
_____
_____
_____
_____
_____
_____

Day 5: _____
_____
_____
_____
_____
_____
_____
_____
_____

Day 6: _____
_____
_____
_____
_____
_____
_____
_____
_____

Day 7: _____
_____
_____
_____
_____
_____
_____
_____
_____

Prayer Needs/Requests & How God Responded: _____

_____

_____

_____

_____

_____

_____

_____

_____

_____

_____

_____

_____

_____

_____

Notes From This Week's Fellowship/Teaching: _____

_____

_____

_____

_____

_____

_____

_____

_____

_____

_____

_____

_____

_____

_____

_____

_____

_____

_____

_____

_____

_____

_____

_____

_____

Personal Accountability Checklist: (if in a group, have someone else check you)
- [ ] I completed the character or command promise study.
- [ ] I read a chapter from the Book Of Proverbs each day.
- [ ] I journaled each day.

Lesson 51: The Commandment To Live And Speak Truth In Love To Brothers

1. **Make Peace With Others:** "Therefore, if you are offering your gift at the altar and there remember that your brother has something against you, leave your gift there in front of the altar. First go and be reconciled to your brother; then come and offer your gift." Matthew 5:23-24

2. **Don't Look Down On The Immature:** "See that you do not look down on one of these little ones. For I tell you that their angels in heaven always see the face of my Father in Heaven." Matthew 18:10

3. **Restore Others In Love, Resolve Offences:** "If your brother sins against you, go and show him his fault, just between the two of you. If he listens to you, you have won your brother over. But if he will not listen, take one or two others along, so that every matter may be established by the testimony of two or three witnesses. If he refuses to listen to them, tell it to the church; and if he refuses to listen even to the church, treat him as you would a pagan or a tax collector." Matthew 18:15-17

4. **Forgive Instead Of Condemning:** "Do not judge, and you will not be judged. Do not condemn, and you will not be condemned. Forgive, and you will be forgiven." Luke 6:37

5. **Forgive Those Who Repent:** "So, watch yourselves. If your brother sins, rebuke him, and if he repents, forgive him." Luke 17:3-4 "Jesus answered, 'I tell you, (forgive) not seven times, but seventy-seven times.' " Matthew 18:22

6. **Evaluate All Things Righteously:** "Stop judging by mere appearances, and make a right judgment." John 7:24 "Do not judge, or you too will be judged. For in the same way you judge others, you will be judged, and with the measure you use, it will be measured to you." Matthew 7:1-2

7. **Love Each Other As Jesus Did:** "My command is this: Love each other as I have loved you." John 15:12

Promises To One Who Gives Generously

1. **Secret Giving Brings Our Father's Rewards:** "But when you give to the needy, do not let your left hand know what your right hand is doing, so that your giving may be in secret. Then your Father, who sees what is done in secret, will reward you." Matthew 6:3-4

2. **Your Giving Measure Becomes Your Receiving Measure:** "Give, and it will be given to you. A good measure, pressed down, shaken together and running over, will be poured into your lap. For with the measure you use, it will be measured to you." Luke 6:38

3. **Giving To The Poor Is A Cleansing Agent:** "But give what is inside the dish to the poor, and everything will be clean for you." Luke 11:41

4. **Give To Become Eternally Welcomed:** "I tell you, use worldly wealth to gain friends for yourselves, so that when it is gone, you will be welcomed into eternal dwellings." Luke 16:9

5. **Giving Brings More Blessings Than Receiving Does:** "In everything I did, I showed you that by this kind of hard work we must help the weak, remembering the words the Lord Jesus himself said: 'It is more blessed to give than to receive.' " Acts 20:35

6. **God Blesses At The Resurrection For Those Who Cannot:** "But when you give a banquet, invite the poor, the crippled, the lame, the blind, and you will be blessed. Although they cannot repay you, you will be repaid at the resurrection of the righteous." Luke 14:13-14

7. **Giving To The Poor And Following Jesus Brings Heavenly Treasure:** " '...One thing you lack,' he said. 'Go, sell everything you have and give to the poor, and you will have treasure in heaven. Then come, follow me.' " Mark 10: 21

Day 1: _____
_____
_____
_____
_____
_____
_____
_____
_____
_____
_____
_____

Day 2: _____
_____
_____
_____
_____
_____
_____
_____
_____
_____
_____
_____

Day 3: _____
_____
_____
_____
_____
_____
_____
_____
_____
_____
_____
_____

Words Of Wisdom: read a chapter from the Book of Proverbs corresponding with today's date (if today is the seventh, read chapter seven from the Book of Proverbs.)

Thus it is written, and thus it behoved Christ to suffer, and to rise from the dead the third day: And that repentance and remission of sins should be preached in his name among all nations, beginning at Jerusalem. And you are witnesses of these things. Luke 24:46-48

Day 4: _____

_____

_____

_____

_____

_____

_____

_____

_____

Day 5: _____

_____

_____

_____

_____

_____

_____

_____

_____

Day 6: _____

_____

_____

_____

_____

_____

_____

_____

_____

Day 7: _____

_____

_____

_____

_____

_____

_____

_____

_____

Prayer Needs/Requests & How God Responded: _____

_____
_____
_____
_____
_____
_____
_____
_____
_____
_____
_____
_____
_____
_____
_____
_____

Notes From This Week's Fellowship/Teaching: _____

_____
_____
_____
_____
_____
_____
_____
_____
_____
_____
_____
_____
_____
_____
_____
_____
_____
_____
_____
_____
_____
_____
_____
_____
_____
_____
_____
_____

Personal Accountability Checklist: (if in a group, have someone else check you)

- ☐ I completed the character or command promise study.
- ☐ I read a chapter from the Book Of Proverbs each day.
- ☐ I journaled each day.

Lesson 52: The Commandment To Finish The Course

1. **When Insulted, Persecuted, Lied About Because Of Jesus, Rejoice:** "Blessed are you when people insult you, persecute you and falsely say all kinds of evil against you because of me. Rejoice and be glad, because great is your reward in heaven, for in the same way they persecuted the prophets who were before you." Matthew 5:11-12 "Rejoice in that day and leap for joy, because great is your reward in heaven. For that is how their fathers treated the prophets." Luke 6:23

2. **Don't Worry About What To Say:** "But when they arrest you, do not worry about what to say or how to say it. At that time you will be given what to say." Matthew 10:19

3. **Traveling Ministers Are To Leave When Persecuted:** "When you are persecuted in one place, flee to another. I tell you the truth, you will not finish going through the cities of Israel before the Son of Man comes." Matthew 10:23

4. **When Severity Comes, Look For Your Nearby Redeemer:** "When these things begin to take place, stand up and lift up your heads, because your redemption is drawing near." Luke 21:28

5. **Stop Grumbling:** " 'Stop grumbling among yourselves,' Jesus answered." John 6:43

6. **Do Not Fear Suffering Or Persecution, Receive Your Crown:** "Do not be afraid of what you are about to suffer. I tell you, the devil will put some of you in prison to test you, and you will suffer persecution for ten days. Be faithful, even to the point of death, and I will give you the crown of life." Revelation 2:10

7. **Hold On To Your Faith, Protect Your Crown:** "I am coming soon. Hold on to what you have, so that no one will take your crown." Revelation 3:11

Promises To The One Who Does Not Yield But Conquers Sin

1. **Overcomers Will Eat Of The Paradise Tree Of Life:** "He who has an ear, let him hear what the Spirit says to the churches. To him who overcomes, I will give the right to eat from the tree of life, which is in the paradise of God." Revelation 2:7

2. **Overcomers Will Not Be Hurt By The Second Death:** "He who has an ear, let him hear what the Spirit says to the churches. He who overcomes will not be hurt at all by the second death." Revelation 2:22

3. **Overcomers Receive Hidden Manna And A New Name:** "He who has an ear, let him hear what the Spirit says to the churches. To him who overcomes, I will give some of the hidden manna. I will also give him a white stone with a new name written on it, known only to him who receives it. " Revelation 2:17

4. **Overcomers Receive Authority Over Nations:** "To him who overcomes and does my will to the end, I will give authority over the nations. 'He will rule them with an iron scepter; he will dash them to pieces like pottery' – just as I have received authority from my Father. I will also give him the morning star." Revelation 2:26-28

5. **Overcomers Will Be Acknowledged Before Our Father And Angels:** "He who overcomes will, like them, be dressed in white. I will never blot out his name from the book of life, but will acknowledge his name before my Father and his angels." Revelation 3:5

6. **Overcomers Will Become Pillars In God's Temple Never To Leave:** "Him who overcomes I will make a pillar in the temple of my God. Never again will he leave it. I will write on him the name of my God and the name of the city of my God, the New Jerusalem, which is coming down out of heaven from my God; and I will also write on him my new name." Revelation 3:12

7. **Overcomers Will Sit With Jesus On His Throne:** "To him who overcomes, I will give the right to sit with me on my throne, just as I overcame and sat down with my Father on his throne." Revelation 3:21

Day 1: _____
_____
_____
_____
_____
_____
_____
_____
_____
_____
_____
_____
_____

Day 2: _____
_____
_____
_____
_____
_____
_____
_____
_____
_____
_____
_____
_____
_____

Day 3: _____
_____
_____
_____
_____
_____
_____
_____
_____
_____
_____
_____
_____
_____

Words Of Wisdom: read a chapter from the Book of Proverbs corresponding with today's date (if today is the seventh, read chapter seven from the Book of Proverbs.)

And, lo, I am with you always, even unto the end of the world. Amen. Mth. 28:19-20.

Day 4: _____
_____
_____
_____
_____
_____
_____
_____
_____

Day 5: _____
_____
_____
_____
_____
_____
_____
_____
_____

Day 6: _____
_____
_____
_____
_____
_____
_____
_____
_____

Day 7: _____
_____
_____
_____
_____
_____
_____
_____
_____

Prayer Needs/Requests & How God Responded: _____

_____

_____

_____

_____

_____

_____

_____

_____

_____

_____

_____

_____

_____

Notes From This Week's Fellowship/Teaching: _____

_____

_____

_____

_____

_____

_____

_____

_____

_____

_____

_____

_____

_____

_____

_____

_____

_____

_____

_____

_____

_____

_____

_____

_____

_____

_____

Personal Accountability Checklist: (if in a group, have someone else check you)

- ☐ I completed the character or command promise study.
- ☐ I read a chapter from the Book Of Proverbs each day.
- ☐ I journaled each day.